INTERMEDIATE 2

HISTORY
2006-2010

2006 EXAM – page 3
2007 EXAM – page 35
2008 EXAM – page 67
2009 EXAM – page 99
2010 EXAM – page 131

© Scottish Qualifications Authority
All rights reserved. Copying prohibited. No part of this publication may be reproduced, stored in a retrieval system, or transmitted in any form or by any means, electronic, mechanical, photocopying, recording or otherwise.

First exam published in 2006.
Published by Bright Red Publishing Ltd, 6 Stafford Street, Edinburgh EH3 7AU
tel: 0131 220 5804 fax: 0131 220 6710 info@brightredpublishing.co.uk www.brightredpublishing.co.uk

ISBN 978-1-84948-123-6

A CIP Catalogue record for this book is available from the British Library.

Bright Red Publishing is grateful to the copyright holders, as credited on the final page of the book, for permission to use their material.
Every effort has been made to trace the copyright holders and to obtain their permission for the use of copyright material.
Bright Red Publishing will be happy to receive information allowing us to rectify any error or omission in future editions.

INTERMEDIATE 2
2006

[BLANK PAGE]

X044/201

NATIONAL
QUALIFICATIONS
2006

MONDAY, 22 MAY
9.00 AM – 10.45 AM

HISTORY
INTERMEDIATE 2

The instructions for this paper are on *Page two*. Read them carefully before you begin your answers.
Some sources in this examination have been adapted or translated.

INSTRUCTIONS

Answer **one** question from Part 1, The Short Essay

Answer **one** context from Part 2, Scottish and British

Answer **one** context from Part 3, European and World

Answer **one** other context from

    either Part 2, Scottish and British

    or   Part 3, European and World

Contents

Part 1 Short Essay Questions.
Answer **one** question only.   Pages 4–6

Part 2 Scottish and British Contexts

1. Murder in the Cathedral: Crown, Church and People, 1154–1173   Page 8
2. Wallace, Bruce and the Wars of Independence, 1286–1328   Page 9
3. Mary, Queen of Scots and the Scottish Reformation, 1540s–1587   Page 10
4. The Coming of the Civil War, 1603–1642   Page 11
5. "Ane End of Ane Auld Sang": Scotland and the Treaty of Union, 1690s–1715   Page 12
6. Immigrants and Exiles: Scotland, 1830s–1930s   Page 13
7.(a) From the Cradle to the Grave? Social Welfare in Britain, 1890s–1951   Page 14

OR

7.(b) Campaigning for Change: Social Change in Scotland, 1900s–1979   Page 15
8. A Time of Troubles: Ireland, 1900–1923   Page 16

Part 3 European and World Contexts

1. The Norman Conquest, 1060–1153   Page 17
2. The Cross and the Crescent: The First Crusade, 1096–1125   Page 18
3. War, Death and Revolt in Medieval Europe, 1328–1436   Page 19
4. New Worlds: Europe in the Age of Expansion, 1480s–1530s   Page 20
5. "Tea and Freedom": The American Revolution, 1763–1783   Page 21
6. "This Accursed Trade": The British Slave Trade and its Abolition, 1770–1807   Page 22
7. Citizens! The French Revolution, 1789–1794   Page 23
8. Cavour, Garibaldi and the Making of Italy, 1815–1870   Page 24
9. Iron and Blood? Bismarck and the Creation of the German Empire, 1815–1871   Page 25
10. The Red Flag: Lenin and the Russian Revolution, 1894–1921   Page 26
11. Free at Last? Race Relations in the USA, 1918–1968   Page 27
12. The Road to War, 1933–1939   Page 28
13. In the Shadow of the Bomb: The Cold War, 1945–1985   Page 29

[Turn over

PART 1: THE SHORT ESSAY

Answer **one** question. For this question you should write a short essay using your own knowledge. The essay should include an introduction, development and conclusion. Each question is worth 8 marks.

SCOTTISH AND BRITISH CONTEXTS:

CONTEXT 1: MURDER IN THE CATHEDRAL: CROWN, CHURCH AND PEOPLE, 1154–1173

Question 1: Explain why monasteries were important in the twelfth century. **8**

CONTEXT 2: WALLACE, BRUCE AND THE WARS OF INDEPENDENCE, 1286–1328

Question 2: Explain why the Scots asked King Edward of England to help them after the death of King Alexander III. **8**

CONTEXT 3: MARY, QUEEN OF SCOTS AND THE SCOTTISH REFORMATION, 1540s–1587

Question 3: Explain why religion was such a serious problem for Mary, Queen of Scots. **8**

CONTEXT 4: THE COMING OF THE CIVIL WAR, 1603–1642

Question 4: Explain why Charles I faced serious problems over religion in Scotland. **8**

CONTEXT 5: "ANE END OF ANE AULD SANG": SCOTLAND AND THE TREATY OF UNION, 1690s–1715

Question 5: Explain why the succession problem was important in bringing about the Union. **8**

CONTEXT 6: IMMIGRANTS AND EXILES: SCOTLAND, 1830s–1930s

Question 6: Explain why so many Irish immigrants arrived in Scotland after 1830. **8**

CONTEXT 7(a): FROM THE CRADLE TO THE GRAVE? SOCIAL WELFARE IN BRITAIN, 1890s–1951

Question 7(a): Explain why the Second World War led to improvements to social welfare in Britain. **8**

Marks

CONTEXT 7(*b*): CAMPAIGNING FOR CHANGE: SOCIAL CHANGE IN SCOTLAND, 1900s–1979

Question 7(*b*): Explain why the Second World War was responsible for changing the working lives of Scottish women.

8

CONTEXT 8: A TIME OF TROUBLES: IRELAND, 1900–1923

Question 8: Explain why civil war broke out in Ireland in 1922.

8

EUROPEAN AND WORLD CONTEXTS:

CONTEXT 1: THE NORMAN CONQUEST, 1060–1153

Question 9: Explain why William of Normandy believed he was the rightful King of England in 1066.

8

CONTEXT 2: THE CROSS AND THE CRESCENT: THE FIRST CRUSADE, 1096–1125

Question 10: Explain why people wanted to go on the First Crusade.

8

CONTEXT 3: WAR, DEATH AND REVOLT IN MEDIEVAL EUROPE, 1328–1436

Question 11: Explain why the Peasants' Revolt broke out in 1381.

8

CONTEXT 4: NEW WORLDS: EUROPE IN THE AGE OF EXPANSION, 1480s–1530s

Question 12: Explain why Spain took a leading role in voyages of exploration between the 1480s and 1530s.

8

CONTEXT 5: "TEA AND FREEDOM": THE AMERICAN REVOLUTION, 1763–1783

Question 13: Explain why so many other countries became involved in the Revolutionary War by 1780.

8

CONTEXT 6: "THIS ACCURSED TRADE": THE BRITISH SLAVE TRADE AND ITS ABOLITION, 1770–1807

Question 14: Explain why so many people defended the Slave Trade in the eighteenth century.

8

CONTEXT 7: CITIZENS! THE FRENCH REVOLUTION, 1789–1794

Question 15: Explain why Louis XVI was executed. 8

CONTEXT 8: CAVOUR, GARIBALDI AND THE MAKING OF ITALY, 1815–1870

Question 16: Explain why there was a growth of Nationalism in Italy between 1815 and 1848. 8

CONTEXT 9: IRON AND BLOOD? BISMARCK AND THE CREATION OF THE GERMAN EMPIRE, 1815–1871

Question 17: Explain the importance of Bismarck to German unification. 8

CONTEXT 10: THE RED FLAG: LENIN AND THE RUSSIAN REVOLUTION, 1894–1921

Question 18: Explain why Lenin was able to seize power in Russia in October 1917. 8

CONTEXT 11: FREE AT LAST? RACE RELATIONS IN THE USA, 1918–1968

Question 19: Explain why American attitudes towards new immigrants changed during the 1920s. 8

CONTEXT 12: THE ROAD TO WAR, 1933–1939

Question 20: Explain why the British Government wanted to avoid war in the 1930s. 8

CONTEXT 13: IN THE SHADOW OF THE BOMB: THE COLD WAR, 1945–1985

Question 21: Explain why the USA and the Soviet Union did not trust each other after World War Two. 8

[END OF PART 1: THE SHORT ESSAY]

[Turn over for PART 2: SCOTTISH AND BRITISH CONTEXTS on *Page eight*]

PART 2:

HISTORICAL STUDY: SCOTTISH AND BRITISH

CONTEXT 1: MURDER IN THE CATHEDRAL: CROWN, CHURCH AND PEOPLE, 1154–1173

Answer the following questions using recalled knowledge and information from the sources where appropriate.

Source A is about the knights' Code of Chivalry.

Source A

> Although knights were men of war they were expected to obey the Code of Chivalry and behave in a courteous and civil way. A true knight had to show mercy to a defeated enemy but would never forgive an insult to himself or someone under his protection. The Church liked the idea of these rules and made the knighting ceremony a religious occasion. In return, knights had to fight against non-Christians.

1. Why did the Code of Chivalry improve the way a knight was expected to behave? (Use **Source A** and recall.) **5**

Source B describes how Becket changed when he became Archbishop of Canterbury. It is taken from the Chronicle of Herbert of Bosham, written in 1184.

Source B

> After Thomas became Archbishop he turned from the power of the king and followed Christ. He wore a hair shirt of the roughest kind next to his skin. It reached to his knees and was covered in lice. He ate as little as possible and drank stale water. Becket no longer kept company with the barons, preferring instead to spend time with the poor of his parish.

Source C also describes how Becket changed when he became Archbishop of Canterbury. It was written by a modern historian.

Source C

> To the king's amazement, Becket stopped thinking of himself as the king's official and began thinking of himself as Christ's ambassador. Previously as chancellor, Becket had been the most splendidly dressed man in the kingdom. Now as Archbishop he wore a rough robe and made a point of washing the feet of the dirtiest beggars. He no longer held feasts and gave up drinking wine.

2. How far do **Sources B** and **C** agree about how Becket changed when he became Archbishop of Canterbury? **4**

3. Describe the murder of Becket in Canterbury Cathedral in 1170. **5**

[END OF CONTEXT 1]

Marks

HISTORICAL STUDY: SCOTTISH AND BRITISH

CONTEXT 2: WALLACE, BRUCE AND THE WARS OF INDEPENDENCE, 1286–1328

Answer the following questions using recalled knowledge and information from the sources where appropriate.

1. Describe the events that led to the defeat and capture of King John Balliol. **5**

Source A describes the Battle of Stirling Bridge.

Source A

> Late in the morning, the standard bearers of the king and the earl crossed the bridge. When the enemy saw that they could win, they soon came down from the hill and they seized the end of the bridge so that no-one could use it. Many were thrown from the bridge and drowned. Cressingham died among the Scots.

Source B also describes the Battle of Stirling Bridge.

Source B

> The Scots allowed as many of the English to cross the bridge as they could hope to defeat, and then, having blocked the bridge, they slaughtered all who had crossed over. Among those who perished was Cressingham. De Warenne escaped with difficulty and with a small following.

2. How far do **Sources A** and **B** agree about what happened at the Battle of Stirling Bridge? **4**

Source C is about what happened when Bruce made himself King of Scots in 1306.

Source C

> The problem which faced many Scots in 1306 should not be under-estimated. Ever since 1297 Scottish patriots had fought for King John Balliol. Many were reluctant to throw Balliol aside and to accept Robert Bruce in his place. To them, Bruce had no right to the throne and he had not always supported Scottish independence. The civil war between Bruce and Balliol divided the Scots more than anything else had in the past.

3. Why were the Scots divided about supporting Bruce or Balliol in 1306? (Use **Source C** and recall.) **5**

[END OF CONTEXT 2]

HISTORICAL STUDY: SCOTTISH AND BRITISH

CONTEXT 3: MARY, QUEEN OF SCOTS AND THE SCOTTISH REFORMATION, 1540s–1587

Answer the following questions using recalled knowledge and information from the sources where appropriate.

1. Describe the events which led to the assassination of Cardinal Beaton at St Andrews in 1546. **5**

Source A explains why events surrounding Queen Mary's marriage to Bothwell led to her downfall.

Source A

> Some nobles used Bothwell to get rid of the king, and planned to use him to ruin the queen. Their plan was to persuade her to marry Bothwell. After that, they intended to accuse her of being involved in her husband's death because she had married the murderer. This poor young princess, inexperienced in such matters, was tricked by everyone around her.

2. Why did Mary's marriage to Bothwell lead to her downfall? (Use **Source A** and recall.) **5**

Source B describes Mary's involvement in the Babington Plot in 1585.

Source B

> Mary enjoyed the excitement of plotting and sending coded letters hidden in a beer keg to Babington. Elizabeth's men knew about the plot from the beginning because they had a spy in Mary's household. The end came when Mary sent a letter enthusiastically approving the assassination of Elizabeth. When the letter was decoded, the spy drew a gallows on the letter.

Source C describes Mary's involvement in the Babington Plot in 1585.

Source C

> Every detail of Babington's plot was known to Elizabeth's government because they knew about the secret letters hidden in the beer kegs. They were waiting for Mary to fall into the trap they had laid for her by agreeing to Elizabeth's murder. Mary mentioned it in her reply but concentrated on the practical details of the plot. This was enough and it was little wonder Elizabeth's man drew a gallows on the letter when he read it.

3. How far do **Sources B** and **C** agree about Mary's involvement in the Babington Plot? **4**

[END OF CONTEXT 3]

HISTORICAL STUDY: SCOTTISH AND BRITISH

CONTEXT 4: THE COMING OF THE CIVIL WAR, 1603–1642

Answer the following questions using recalled knowledge and information from the sources where appropriate.

In **Source A** James VI and I states his views on the nature of kingship.

Source A

> For I tell you this, the State of monarchy is the most supreme thing on all the earth. This power is given to kings by God. It is well known that kings are not only God's lieutenants on earth, but even by God Himself they are called gods.

In **Source B** the modern historian M. M. Reese describes James VI and I's view of kingship.

Source B

> James was totally convinced that he had a God given right to rule. His writings proclaimed, and his actions constantly showed, that kings were not restricted by any laws made by men. He believed kings were responsible to God alone and were His anointed servants, equal to gods.

1. How far do **Sources A** and **B** agree about James VI and I's belief in the Divine Right of Kings? **4**

2. Describe Charles I's attempts to finance his government without Parliament 1629–1640. **5**

Source C describes the reasons for parliamentary opposition to the king by the time of the Long Parliament.

Source C

> Many county gentry coming to the Long Parliament felt that it might be the last chance to prevent England becoming a Roman Catholic-dominated, absolutist state. Much of their fear centred on Strafford whose record in Ireland and in the Council of the North showed him to be a ruthless minister who could make absolutism work.

3. Why did many people in the Long Parliament oppose the king? (Use **Source C** and recall.) **5**

[END OF CONTEXT 4]

HISTORICAL STUDY: SCOTTISH AND BRITISH

CONTEXT 5: "ANE END OF ANE AULD SANG": SCOTLAND AND THE TREATY OF UNION, 1690s–1715

Answer the following questions using recalled knowledge and information from the sources where appropriate.

Source A is about the Worcester incident in 1705.

Source A

> The Worcester incident was a savage flare up of anti-English feeling in Scotland. The Scots believed that Captain Green of the Worcester had sunk a Scottish ship. Rumours that Green and his men would be set free by the Queen's orders angered the Edinburgh mob which threatened to execute the prisoners. This anger was provoked by a host of reasons including memories of the Darien Expedition and resentment about the effects of England's wars on Scotland's trade with France.

1. Why was there bad feeling between Scotland and England in 1705? (Use **Source A** and recall.) **5**

Source B is a description of Scottish reaction to the plans for a Union in 1706 written by a Scottish opponent of the Union.

Source B

> If we made a tour of the country we would find an even greater dislike of the Union than in Edinburgh. People flocked to protest about the Union and to express their resentment, voicing their displeasure with the greatest indignation. Since they could not tell their representatives what they thought in person, they decided that signing a petition was the best way to protest about taking away their Parliament.

Source C is from a report by Daniel Defoe, an English spy sent to Scotland in 1706.

Source C

> I had not been in Edinburgh for long when I heard a great noise and, looking out, I saw a terrible mob coming up the High Street led by a drummer. They were shouting and swearing and crying out "all Scotland will stand together!", "No Union! No Union!", "English dogs" and things like that.

2. Compare **Sources B** and **C** as evidence about Scottish attitudes to the Union. **4**

3. In what ways did the passing of the Act of Union help the Jacobite Cause? **5**

[END OF CONTEXT 5]

HISTORICAL STUDY: SCOTTISH AND BRITISH

CONTEXT 6: IMMIGRANTS AND EXILES: SCOTLAND, 1830s–1930s

Answer the following questions using recalled knowledge and information from the sources where appropriate.

Source A comments on the experience of Irish immigrants in Scotland.

Source A

> During the nineteenth century a number of Scots criticised Irish people for their behaviour. Newspapers drew attention to violent events in which Irish people were involved. Reporters often used words like "vicious" to describe Irish people involved in fights and crimes. Irish navvies building railways were shown as especially violent, although Scots and English were as bad. In 1836, police superintendents said that Irish people were more likely to steal, beg and fight than Scots.

1. Why did many Scots dislike Irish immigrants in Scotland? (Use **Source A** and recall.) **5**

Source B is about Scottish emigration to Canada.

Source B

> Civilian emigration to Canada was encouraged by the problems caused to the crofter's way of life by improvements on Highland estates. It was also caused by the overpopulation of the area and crop failures. The Government established an Emigration Commission which issued advice to would-be emigrants.

Source C is about emigration from the Highlands of Scotland.

Source C

> For much of the nineteenth century emigration was seen as a solution to overpopulation in the Highlands. In the 1850s funds were raised by the Highland and Island Emigration Society to relieve distress during the potato famine. It helped send emigrants to Australia. The British and Canadian governments set up the Crofter Colonisation Scheme, which was intended to reduce overpopulation in the crofting areas and to settle the Canadian prairies.

2. How far do **Sources B** and **C** agree about emigration from Scotland? **4**

3. What difficulties faced Scots in the countries to which they emigrated? **5**

[END OF CONTEXT 6]

HISTORICAL STUDY: SCOTTISH AND BRITISH

> **CONTEXT 7(a): FROM THE CRADLE TO THE GRAVE? SOCIAL WELFARE IN BRITAIN, 1890s–1951**

Answer the following questions using recalled knowledge and information from the sources where appropriate.

Source A is from a memory of a family in Springburn, Glasgow in the early twentieth century.

Source A

> I had an uncle who was unemployed in the depression. And he'd five kids. He had to walk from Anderston to Barnhill, rain, hail or snow, to chop wood all day for 5s (25p) per week. If he was sick and he couldn't go he got nothing. The kids got nothing.

Source B is from a speech by Lloyd George, a leading Liberal MP in 1906.

Source B

> What are some of the causes of poverty? There is the fact that a man's earnings are not enough to maintain himself and his family. There is the inability to obtain employment for economic reasons. There is the inability of men to work owing to sickness, old age or lack of physical stamina or vitality. Then there is the most fertile cause of all – a man's own habits such as drinking and gambling.

1. How far do **Sources A** and **B** agree about the causes of poverty in the early twentieth century?

Source C explains the need for the Liberal reforms 1906–1914.

Source C

> The first reform passed by the Liberal Government was the provision of school meals for children. The Boer War and the poor condition of many recruits led politicians to act. The children were the soldiers of the future. The need for a healthy workforce also led to the medical inspection of children. Pressure for old age pensions came from a number of places. Most people thought pension payments to the elderly were a good idea. New Zealand and Germany had already introduced pensions.

2. Why did the Liberals introduce reforms for children and the elderly? (Use **Source C** and recall.)

3. Describe the changes made by the Labour Government after 1945 to create a welfare state.

[END OF CONTEXT 7(a)]

Marks

HISTORICAL STUDY: SCOTTISH AND BRITISH

CONTEXT 7(b): CAMPAIGNING FOR CHANGE: SOCIAL CHANGE IN SCOTLAND, 1900s–1979

Answer the following questions using recalled knowledge and information from the sources where appropriate.

Source A describes attitudes to women's suffrage.

Source A

> When the Women's Social and Political Union began to destroy property and risk the lives of innocent people, the public began to turn against them. The National Union of Women's Suffrage Societies, whose gallant educational and constitutional work for women's freedom had been carried on for more than fifty years, publicly condemned these terrorist activities.

Source B also describes attitudes to women's suffrage.

Source B

> The window smashing has aroused great hostility against the suffragettes. Because of the responsible campaign by the women's movement everything was looking favourable for a change in the law to grant women the vote. The last outbreak has however endangered everything. I am now certain that all intelligent women must reject the methods of the Pankhursts.

1. How far do **Sources A** and **B** agree about the effects of suffragette violence on public opinion? **4**

2. Describe popular entertainment in the 1920s. **5**

Source C explains the importance of gas and oil for Scotland in the 1970s.

Source C

> The benefits to the nation of oil and gas exploitation include improved employment in the North East and increased government income through taxation. There will be new job opportunities in oil-related technology and in the support industries to service oil rigs. Future prospects for new fields are uncertain but exploratory drilling will continue for some time.

3. Why were the oil and gas industries so important to employment in Scotland in the 1970s? (Use **Source C** and recall.) **5**

[END OF CONTEXT 7(b)]

HISTORICAL STUDY: SCOTTISH AND BRITISH

CONTEXT 8: A TIME OF TROUBLES: IRELAND, 1900–1923

Answer the following questions using recalled knowledge and information from the sources where appropriate.

Source A explains why Unionists were against the Home Rule Bill of 1912.

Source A

> Many Unionists were strongly against the Home Rule Bill. For many the slogan was "Home Rule is Rome Rule" – a belief that the Catholic Church had too much power in Dublin. Unionists were also worried their industry would suffer, as it depended on Britain as a source for raw materials. In Ulster attempts were made to delay the Bill, there was fear that if it were passed it would lead to full independence and destroy their way of life.

1. Why were Unionists opposed to the Home Rule Bill of 1912? (Use **Source A** and recall.)

2. Describe the events of the Easter Rising, 1916.

Source B is a statement by Eamon de Valera and describes reaction to the Anglo-Irish Treaty.

Source B

> I am against this treaty because it does not give Ireland the freedom that it wants. I am against this treaty because it will not end the centuries of fighting between Great Britain and Ireland. They have signed a document that has handed over authority to a foreign country. They have tied us to the British Empire forever.

Source C was written by Arthur Griffith and also describes reaction to the Anglo-Irish Treaty.

Source C

> We were sent to make some compromises, bargain or arrangement and we have done that. This treaty gives the Irish people what they have not had for centuries, freedom. We can make peace on the basis of this treaty. It does not tie us to Britain and does not stop us from asking for more in the future. This treaty gives us the right to rule in our own country.

3. How far do **Sources B** and **C** disagree about reaction to the Anglo-Irish Treaty of 1921?

[END OF CONTEXT 8]

[END OF PART 2: SCOTTISH AND BRITISH CONTEXTS]

Marks

PART 3:

HISTORICAL STUDY: EUROPEAN AND WORLD

CONTEXT 1: THE NORMAN CONQUEST, 1060–1153

Answer the following questions using recalled knowledge and information from the sources where appropriate.

In **Source A** the historian G.W.S. Barrow describes William I's creation of a feudal baronage in England.

Source A

> In every part of the country the king established some of his leading followers as holders of great estates. This was on the specific condition that they would provide the king with a fixed number of knights to serve in his army when required.

1. How useful is **Source A** as evidence of William I's methods of controlling England? 4

2. Describe David I's methods of governing Scotland. 5

Source B is about David I and the Scottish Church.

Source B

> David's mother was considered a saint. David turned his attention to Church matters because he was a religious man. He appointed more Anglo-Norman bishops to bishoprics such as Glasgow, Brechin and Dunblane. The king made administrative reforms by establishing more parishes and set up many monasteries like Melrose and Kelso in the Borders.

3. Why was David I's reign important for the Church in Scotland? (Use **Source B** and recall.) 5

[END OF CONTEXT 1]

HISTORICAL STUDY: EUROPEAN AND WORLD

CONTEXT 2: THE CROSS AND THE CRESCENT: THE FIRST CRUSADE, 1096–1125

Answer the following questions using recalled knowledge and information from the sources where appropriate.

1. Describe the capture of Nicaea by the Crusaders. **5**

Source A was written by Fulcher of Chartres, a priest who went on the First Crusade but was not present at Jerusalem.

Source A

> Our knights split open the bellies of those they had just killed in order to extract from the guts the gold coins which the Muslims had gulped down their loathsome throats whilst alive. Our men ran through the city not sparing anyone and seizing whatever they found. In this way poor men became rich.

2. How useful is **Source A** as evidence of the Crusaders' behaviour during the capture of Jerusalem? **4**

Source B explains why the Crusaders needed to have a strong leader after the capture of Jerusalem.

Source B

> Godfrey of Bouillon was elected to rule in Jerusalem. He refused to take the title of king and instead became known as the "Defender of the Holy City". A ruler was urgently needed to organise an army to protect the city. The Egyptians were advancing on Jerusalem. Under Godfrey's leadership the Crusaders destroyed the Egyptians. Godfrey's next task was to persuade the small crusading army to stay in the East and help build castles needed for defence.

3. Why did the Crusaders need a strong leader after the capture of Jerusalem? (Use **Source B** and recall.) **5**

[END OF CONTEXT 2]

HISTORICAL STUDY: EUROPEAN AND WORLD

CONTEXT 3: WAR, DEATH AND REVOLT IN MEDIEVAL EUROPE, 1328–1436

Answer the following questions using recalled knowledge and information from the sources where appropriate.

Source A is about the Battle of Poitiers in 1356.

Source A

> At Poitiers, the English found much greater resistance than in earlier battles. Edward found a defensive position among the vineyards. The English victory showed the skill of the Black Prince and his officers. With trumpets blowing and cries of "St George" they encircled and defeated the French. Among their 2000 prisoners was King John who was taken to London as a captive.

1. Why was the Battle of Poitiers important in the Hundred Years' War? (Use **Source A** and recall.) **5**

2. Describe the political problems which faced France during the reign of Charles VI. **5**

Source B is taken from *Personal Recollections of Joan of Arc* by her servant Louis de Conte.

Source B

> France was a ruin. Half of it belonged to England. Now came Joan to confront the terrible war that had swept the land for three generations. Then began the briefest and most amazing campaign. At Orleans she struck a staggering blow. At Patay, two thousand English were left dead upon the field. With her little hand, that child struck down the enemy.

3. How useful is **Source B** as evidence about Joan of Arc's role in the victory of France in the Hundred Years' War? **4**

[END OF CONTEXT 3]

HISTORICAL STUDY: EUROPEAN AND WORLD

CONTEXT 4: NEW WORLDS: EUROPE IN THE AGE OF EXPANSION, 1480s–1530s

Answer the following questions using recalled knowledge and information from the sources where appropriate.

Source A is about Henry the Navigator of Portugal.

Source A

> Prince Henry was a most Christian prince whose faith urged him to do great deeds. He wanted knowledge of the lands beyond the Canaries because no-one knew anything about them. He had a great wish to learn the full extent of Muslim power in Africa and to spread Christianity amongst the peoples of that land.

1. Why did Henry the Navigator encourage voyages of exploration? (Use **Source A** and recall.)

2. Describe da Gama's first voyage to India.

Source B was written by a soldier in a Conquistador army of the 1520s.

Source B

> We went to serve God and His Majesty the King of Spain, to give light to those who were in darkness and to grow rich as all men desire to do.

3. How useful is **Source B** as evidence of why Spaniards joined the Conquistadors?

[END OF CONTEXT 4]

HISTORICAL STUDY: EUROPEAN AND WORLD

CONTEXT 5: "TEA AND FREEDOM": THE AMERICAN REVOLUTION, 1763–1783

Answer the following questions using recalled knowledge and information from the sources where appropriate.

1. What crimes did the colonists accuse George III of having committed against them by 1776? **5**

In **Source A** a British officer, Lieutenant Mackenzie, describes events at Lexington.

Source A

> Our men had very few opportunities of getting good shots at the rebels who hardly ever fired unless they had the cover of a stone wall, from behind a tree or out by the cover of a house. The moment they fired they lay down out of sight until they loaded their rifles again. What an unfair method of carrying on a war!

2. How useful is **Source A** as evidence of the difficulties faced by the British troops fighting in America? **4**

Source B explains the importance of events at Saratoga in the war.

Source B

> The tactic was for Burgoyne's army to march down to Albany and control the Hudson valley with other British armies. Although he had some success, things went quickly wrong. Facing many difficulties, he retreated to Saratoga where a larger colonial force defeated him. Saratoga was a disaster for Britain because not only did it give the American forces new heart, it encouraged France, then Spain, to enter the war.

3. Why was Saratoga a turning point in the war? (Use **Source B** and recall.) **5**

[END OF CONTEXT 5]

HISTORICAL STUDY: EUROPEAN AND WORLD

CONTEXT 6: "THIS ACCURSED TRADE": THE BRITISH SLAVE TRADE AND ITS ABOLITION, 1770–1807

Answer the following questions using recalled knowledge and information from the sources where appropriate.

Source A is from a description in 1789 by a former slave, Olaudah Equiano, of his experiences during the Middle Passage.

Source A

> I can now tell of the hardships which cannot be separated from this accursed trade. The wretched conditions below decks were made worse by the chains. The shrieks of women, and the groans of the dying, rendered the whole scene one of unimaginable horror.

1. How useful is **Source A** as evidence of the treatment of slaves during the Middle Passage? **4**

2. Describe the methods used by the Abolitionists. **5**

Source B explains why the need for the slave trade changed.

Source B

> Despite the belief that the slave trade was vital, views did begin to change by the late eighteenth century. In Europe and America demand grew to end the cruel slave trade. More and more people began to think of Africans as fellow human beings. Britain at this time was changing from a farming to an industrial country. Her trading interests were also changing. The "sugar island" colonies became less important.

3. Why did the need for the slave trade decline by the late eighteenth century? (Use **Source B** and recall.) **5**

[END OF CONTEXT 6]

HISTORICAL STUDY: EUROPEAN AND WORLD

CONTEXT 7: CITIZENS! THE FRENCH REVOLUTION, 1789–1794

Answer the following questions using recalled knowledge and information from the sources where appropriate.

Source A was written by Arthur Young, a British visitor to France, in July 1789.

Source A

> I have been witness to a scene strange to a foreigner. On passing through the square of the Hotel de Ville, the mob were breaking windows with stones even though there were soldiers stationed there.

1. How useful is **Source A** as evidence of the behaviour of French citizens in 1789? **4**

2. Describe the ways in which the Constituent Assembly reorganised the government of France by 1791. **5**

Source B is about the setting up of the Committee of Public Safety, in April 1793.

Source B

> There will be formed, by open vote, a Committee of Public Safety. The committee will meet in secret and will have the power to suspend the laws of the National Convention if they are against the national interest. In emergency circumstances, the committee shall issue warrants of search and arrest and they shall be obeyed without delay.

3. Why did so many people live in fear in France in 1793? (Use **Source B** and recall.) **5**

[END OF CONTEXT 7]

HISTORICAL STUDY: EUROPEAN AND WORLD

CONTEXT 8: CAVOUR, GARIBALDI AND THE MAKING OF ITALY, 1815–1870

Answer the following questions using recalled knowledge and information from the sources where appropriate.

Source A is from a speech by Cavour to the Piedmontese Parliament in July 1853.

Source A

> Millions of lira* have been spent on new railways. This year ten million lira will be spent on new roads in Sardinia. Hundreds of millions have been spent to make Genoa one of the greatest commercial centres in Europe. If we continue down this road with energy, wisdom and firmness it will lead this brave nation to a great future.

*Lira: Italian money

1. How useful is **Source A** as evidence about the modernisation of Piedmont?

Source B explains British attitudes to Italian unification.

Source B

> The Prime Minister, Palmerston, and his Foreign Secretary, Russell, were keen to see the creation of a united Italy, but not all British politicians agreed. The balance of power in Europe was shifting. They were determined that this should not result in increased foreign domination of the Italian peninsula. If Italy became a united country it would assist the balance of power in Europe. British leaders were keen to see the creation of a more liberal Europe.

2. Why were many people in Britain sympathetic towards Italian unification? (Use **Source B** and recall.)

3. Describe the contribution of Cavour to Italian unification.

[END OF CONTEXT 8]

Marks

HISTORICAL STUDY: EUROPEAN AND WORLD

CONTEXT 9: IRON AND BLOOD? BISMARCK AND THE CREATION OF THE GERMAN EMPIRE, 1815–1871

Answer the following questions using recalled knowledge and information from the sources where appropriate.

Source A is from a speech made by a student at Leipzig in 1820.

Source A

> We are an enthusiastic people who are willing to fight for such laws and for liberty and so the Fatherland cannot be conquered. We are all Germans together made equal through speech and customs, all citizens of Germany. A unified people is irresistible.

1. How useful is **Source A** as evidence about nationalist feeling in the German states after 1815? **4**

Source B is about the failure of the Frankfurt Parliament in 1849.

Source B

> When the princes made clear their refusal to accept the resolutions of the Frankfurt Parliament, the parliamentarians themselves had no other plan in mind. They did not want to lead a revolt against the princes whose power remained strong. Once the revolutions in Vienna and Berlin had been crushed it was only a matter of time before the Frankfurt Parliament failed.

2. Why did the Frankfurt Parliament fail? (Use **Source B** and recall.) **5**

3. Describe the dealings between Bismarck and the Prussian Parliament, 1862–1871. **5**

[END OF CONTEXT 9]

HISTORICAL STUDY: EUROPEAN AND WORLD

CONTEXT 10: THE RED FLAG: LENIN AND THE RUSSIAN REVOLUTION, 1894–1921

Answer the following questions using recalled knowledge and information from the sources where appropriate.

Source A explains the importance of the Orthodox Church in Tsarist Russia.

Source A

> In most houses there were holy pictures on the walls. Holy men or "startsy" were held in special regard. However, there was a great gap between the parish priests on the one side and the bishops and higher clergy on the other. The Orthodox Church was closely linked to the Tsar and supported his way of ruling.

1. Why was the Orthodox Church important in Tsarist Russia? (Use **Source A** and recall.)   5

Source B is from a statement by Rodzianko, President of the Duma, in 1916.

Source B

> What can one do when all the ministers and most of the people in close contact with the Tsar are the tools of Rasputin? The only solution is to kill the scoundrel but there is not a man in Russia who has the guts to do it. If I weren't so old I would do it myself.

2. How useful is **Source B** as evidence of concern about Rasputin's influence over the government of Tsarist Russia?   4

3. Describe Lenin's return to Russia in April 1917.   5

[END OF CONTEXT 10]

HISTORICAL STUDY: EUROPEAN AND WORLD

CONTEXT 11: FREE AT LAST? RACE RELATIONS IN THE USA, 1918–1968

Answer the following questions using recalled knowledge and information from the sources where appropriate.

Source A shows members of the Ku Klux Klan marching in Washington DC in 1926.

Source A

1. How useful is **Source A** as evidence of the activities of the Ku Klux Klan between the First and Second World Wars? **4**

Source B is about the march on Washington in 1963.

Source B

> More than thirty Freedom Trains and 2000 Freedom Buses were hired to take marchers to the capital city. Marchers assembled in front of the Lincoln Memorial in the capital city of the USA. Many of the marchers were African Americans, but about 20 per cent of the crowd was made up of White marchers who were demonstrating their support for the Civil Rights Movement. The demonstration was peaceful and orderly.

2. Why was the march on Washington important for the Civil Rights Movement? (Use **Source B** and recall.) **5**

3. In what ways did the Civil Rights Campaigns change the lives of Black Americans? **5**

[END OF CONTEXT 11]

HISTORICAL STUDY: EUROPEAN AND WORLD

CONTEXT 12: THE ROAD TO WAR, 1933–1939

Answer the following questions using recalled knowledge and information from the sources where appropriate.

Source A is about the agreements Germany made with other countries by 1937.

Source A

> By 1937 Hitler had ensured that Germany was in a much stronger position. The Anglo-German Naval Agreement of 1935 said that Germany could have a navy one third the size of Britain's fleet. By October 1936 a secret agreement had been made by which Germany and Italy agreed to work closer together. A month later Germany and Japan signed an anti-Communist Treaty, which Italy also signed the following year.

1. Why was Germany in a stronger international position by 1937? (Use **Source A** and recall.) **5**

2. Describe the events leading to the Anschluss with Austria in March 1938. **5**

Source B is part of Neville Chamberlain's radio broadcast to the British people during the Czech crisis on 27th September 1938.

Source B

> How terrible, fantastic, incredible it is that we should be digging trenches and trying on gas masks here because of a quarrel in a far away country between people of whom we know nothing.

3. How useful is **Source B** as evidence of the British Government's attitude to the Czech crisis in 1938? **4**

[END OF CONTEXT 12]

HISTORICAL STUDY: EUROPEAN AND WORLD

CONTEXT 13: IN THE SHADOW OF THE BOMB: THE COLD WAR, 1945–1985

Answer the following questions using recalled knowledge and information from the sources where appropriate.

Source A is a speech given by President Kennedy, visiting West Berlin in 1963.

Source A

> There are many people in the world who really don't understand what is the great issue between the free world and the communist world.
> Let them come to Berlin!
> There are some who say in Europe and elsewhere we can work with the communists.
> Let them come to Berlin!
> All free men, wherever they may live, are citizens of Berlin. Therefore, as a free man, I take pride in the words "Ich bin ein Berliner" [I am a Berliner].

1. How useful is **Source A** as evidence of the divisions over Berlin between the USA and the Soviet Union? — 4

2. Describe the results of the Cuban missile crisis in 1962. — 5

Source B explains why people began to oppose the war in Vietnam.

Source B

> In 1968, the Vietcong launched a major new offensive – the Tet Offensive. Although this was a disaster for the Vietcong, the mood in America began to change. The war was being shown on American television and this caused many people to question why they were fighting in Vietnam. News of the atrocities at My Lai also fuelled anti-war feelings of Americans. Peace talks made little progress in Paris.

3. Why were most Americans opposed to the war in Vietnam by 1970? (Use **Source B** and recall.) — 5

[END OF CONTEXT 13]
[END OF PART 3: EUROPEAN AND WORLD CONTEXTS]
[END OF QUESTION PAPER]

INTERMEDIATE 2

2007

[BLANK PAGE]

X044/201

NATIONAL QUALIFICATIONS 2007

FRIDAY, 18 MAY 9.00 AM – 10.45 AM

HISTORY INTERMEDIATE 2

The instructions for this paper are on *Page two*. Read them carefully before you begin your answers. Some sources in this examination have been adapted or translated.

INSTRUCTIONS

Answer **one** question from Part 1, The Short Essay

Answer **one** context from Part 2, Scottish and British

Answer **one** context from Part 3, European and World

Answer **one** other context from

    either Part 2, Scottish and British

    or   Part 3, European and World

Contents

Part 1 Short Essay Questions.
Answer **one** question only. Pages 4–6

Part 2 Scottish and British Contexts

1. Murder in the Cathedral: Crown, Church and People, 1154–1173 — Page 8
2. Wallace, Bruce and the Wars of Independence, 1286–1328 — Page 9
3. Mary, Queen of Scots and the Scottish Reformation, 1540s–1587 — Page 10
4. The Coming of the Civil War, 1603–1642 — Page 11
5. "Ane End of Ane Auld Sang": Scotland and the Treaty of Union, 1690s–1715 — Page 12
6. Immigrants and Exiles: Scotland, 1830s–1930s — Page 13
7.(a) From the Cradle to the Grave? Social Welfare in Britain, 1890s–1951 — Page 14

OR

7.(b) Campaigning for Change: Social Change in Scotland, 1900s–1979 — Page 15
8. A Time of Troubles: Ireland, 1900–1923 — Page 16

Part 3 European and World Contexts

1. The Norman Conquest, 1060–1153 — Page 17
2. The Cross and the Crescent: The First Crusade, 1096–1125 — Page 18
3. War, Death and Revolt in Medieval Europe, 1328–1436 — Page 19
4. New Worlds: Europe in the Age of Expansion, 1480s–1530s — Page 20
5. "Tea and Freedom": The American Revolution, 1763–1783 — Page 21
6. "This Accursed Trade": The British Slave Trade and its Abolition, 1770–1807 — Page 22
7. Citizens! The French Revolution, 1789–1794 — Page 23
8. Cavour, Garibaldi and the Making of Italy, 1815–1870 — Page 24
9. Iron and Blood? Bismarck and the Creation of the German Empire, 1815–1871 — Page 25
10. The Red Flag: Lenin and the Russian Revolution, 1894–1921 — Page 26
11. Free at Last? Race Relations in the USA, 1918–1968 — Page 27
12. The Road to War, 1933–1939 — Page 28
13. In the Shadow of the Bomb: The Cold War, 1945–1985 — Page 29

[Turn over

PART 1: THE SHORT ESSAY

Answer **one** question. For this question you should write a short essay using your own knowledge. The essay should include an introduction, development and conclusion. Each question is worth 8 marks.

SCOTTISH AND BRITISH CONTEXTS:

CONTEXT 1: MURDER IN THE CATHEDRAL: CROWN, CHURCH AND PEOPLE, 1154–1173

Question 1: Explain why Henry II quarrelled with Archbishop Becket. **8**

CONTEXT 2: WALLACE, BRUCE AND THE WARS OF INDEPENDENCE, 1286–1328

Question 2: Explain why Robert Bruce was successful in making himself King of Scots. **8**

CONTEXT 3: MARY, QUEEN OF SCOTS AND THE SCOTTISH REFORMATION, 1540s–1587

Question 3: Explain why Queen Elizabeth ordered the execution of Mary, Queen of Scots in 1587. **8**

CONTEXT 4: THE COMING OF THE CIVIL WAR, 1603–1642

Question 4: Explain why James I quarrelled with the English Parliament during his reign. **8**

CONTEXT 5: "ANE END OF ANE AULD SANG": SCOTLAND AND THE TREATY OF UNION, 1690s–1715

Question 5: Explain why the Scottish colony at Darien failed. **8**

CONTEXT 6: IMMIGRANTS AND EXILES: SCOTLAND, 1830s–1930s

Question 6: Explain why many Scots left to go overseas between the 1830s and 1930s. **8**

CONTEXT 7(a): FROM THE CRADLE TO THE GRAVE? SOCIAL WELFARE IN BRITAIN, 1890s–1951

Question 7(a): Explain why the social reforms of the Liberal government 1906–1914 were important in improving the welfare of the British people. **8**

	Marks
CONTEXT 7(b): CAMPAIGNING FOR CHANGE: SOCIAL CHANGE IN SCOTLAND, 1900s–1979	
Question 7(b): Explain why all women were given the vote by 1928.	8

CONTEXT 8: A TIME OF TROUBLES: IRELAND, 1900–1923	
Question 8: Explain why the Ulster Unionists opposed the Home Rule Bill.	8

EUROPEAN AND WORLD CONTEXTS:

CONTEXT 1: THE NORMAN CONQUEST, 1060–1153	
Question 9: Explain why David I's reign has been called the "Normanisation" of Scotland.	8

CONTEXT 2: THE CROSS AND THE CRESCENT: THE FIRST CRUSADE, 1096–1125	
Question 10: Explain why the People's Crusade failed.	8

CONTEXT 3: WAR, DEATH AND REVOLT IN MEDIEVAL EUROPE, 1328–1436	
Question 11: Explain why Joan of Arc was executed in 1431.	8

CONTEXT 4: NEW WORLDS: EUROPE IN THE AGE OF EXPANSION, 1480s–1530s	
Question 12: Explain why Portugal was able to discover new trade routes to the East in the late fifteenth and early sixteenth centuries.	8

CONTEXT 5: "TEA AND FREEDOM": THE AMERICAN REVOLUTION, 1763–1783	
Question 13: Explain why the defeat of the French in 1763 created tensions in the American colonies.	8

CONTEXT 6: "THIS ACCURSED TRADE": THE BRITISH SLAVE TRADE AND ITS ABOLITION, 1770–1807	
Question 14: Explain why slave resistance on the plantations was mainly unsuccessful.	8

[Turn over

CONTEXT 7: CITIZENS! THE FRENCH REVOLUTION, 1789–1794

Question 15: Explain why the Terror gave Robespierre complete control of France.

CONTEXT 8: CAVOUR, GARIBALDI AND THE MAKING OF ITALY, 1815–1870

Question 16: Explain why Italian unification had not been achieved by 1850.

CONTEXT 9: IRON AND BLOOD? BISMARCK AND THE CREATION OF THE GERMAN EMPIRE, 1815–1871

Question 17: Explain why there was a growth in German nationalism between 1815 and 1850.

CONTEXT 10: THE RED FLAG: LENIN AND THE RUSSIAN REVOLUTION, 1894–1921

Question 18: Explain why there was a revolution in Russia in January 1905.

CONTEXT 11: FREE AT LAST? RACE RELATIONS IN THE USA, 1918–1968

Question 19: Explain why a civil rights movement grew in the USA in the 1950s and 1960s.

CONTEXT 12: THE ROAD TO WAR, 1933–1939

Question 20: Explain why Germany's neighbours felt threatened by Hitler's foreign policy in the period 1933–1938.

CONTEXT 13: IN THE SHADOW OF THE BOMB: THE COLD WAR, 1945–1985

Question 21: Explain why views on the Vietnam War changed in the United States.

[END OF PART 1: THE SHORT ESSAY]

[Turn over for PART 2: SCOTTISH AND BRITISH CONTEXTS on *Page eight*]

PART 2:

HISTORICAL STUDY: SCOTTISH AND BRITISH

CONTEXT 1: MURDER IN THE CATHEDRAL: CROWN, CHURCH AND PEOPLE, 1154–1173

Answer the following questions using recalled knowledge and information from the sources where appropriate.

Source A explains why Henry II had to reform the legal system when he became king in 1154.

Source A

> When Henry became king it ended the brutal twenty-year civil war of Stephen's reign. Henry needed to gain control of his country. During the war the barons had set up their own law courts and were running the law in their own areas. Many barons had also become sheriffs and were corrupt. Although Henry had not been in charge of the country for long he needed to act quickly to remove the barons' armies from the country.

1. Why did Henry II have to reform the legal system when he became king in 1154? (Use **Source A** and recall.)

2. Describe the uses of castles in medieval times.

Source B was written by Abbot Ailred in the twelfth century. It describes life at Rievaulx Abbey in Yorkshire.

Source B

> Our food is simple, our clothes are rough, our drink is from the stream. Under our tired limbs there is only a mat when we sleep; when sleep is sweetest we must rise at a bell's bidding to services. There is no moment of idleness. Everywhere there is peace and a marvellous freedom from the cares of the world.

3. How useful is **Source B** as evidence of the life of a medieval monk?

[END OF CONTEXT 1]

HISTORICAL STUDY: SCOTTISH AND BRITISH

CONTEXT 2: WALLACE, BRUCE AND THE WARS OF INDEPENDENCE, 1286–1328

Answer the following questions using recalled knowledge and information from the sources where appropriate.

Source A is a letter written by Bishop Fraser of St Andrews to King Edward in October 1290.

Source A

> A rumour has spread among the people that the Maid of Norway has died. The Bishop of Durham, Earl Warenne and I then heard that she has recovered from her sickness but that she is very weak. We have agreed to stay at Perth until we hear definite news about her. We have sent two knights to Orkney to find out exactly what has happened.

1. How useful is **Source A** as evidence about what happened while the Scots waited for the arrival of the Maid? **4**

2. Describe what happened at the Battle of Falkirk in 1298. **5**

Source B explains why the Scots had recognised King Edward's authority by 1305.

Source B

> In May 1303 King Edward invaded Scotland once more – but for the last time. He made an armed progress through the realm and stayed for the winter in Dunfermline. Edward then punished the Scottish nobles by making them pay fines. He exiled a few of their most troublesome leaders but there was only one execution. By 1305 King Edward felt he had secured his authority in Scotland.

3. Why did the Scots recognise King Edward's authority by 1305? (Use **Source B** and recall.) **5**

[END OF CONTEXT 2]

HISTORICAL STUDY: SCOTTISH AND BRITISH

CONTEXT 3: MARY, QUEEN OF SCOTS AND THE SCOTTISH REFORMATION, 1540s–1587

Answer the following questions using recalled knowledge and information from the sources where appropriate.

Source A explains why Scottish Protestants rebelled against Mary of Guise in 1559.

Source A

> In 1559, Mary, Queen of Scots, who claimed to be the rightful Queen of England, became Queen of France. This worried the pro-English Protestant nobles. Her mother, Mary of Guise, governed Scotland with the help of an increasing number of French officials and soldiers. At the time when Scottish worries about French control were growing, Mary of Guise began to take action against Protestants in Scotland.

1. Why did Scottish Protestants rebel against Mary of Guise in 1559? (Use **Source A** and recall.) 5

Source B are Queen Mary's orders to pay ministers of the Church of Scotland, issued in 1566.

Source B

> Because the ministers within Scotland have not been paid for this last year and because I determined that they should be paid in the future, I have, with the advice of my government officials, decided to allocate the sum of £10 000 for their payment. I have also ordered that this sum must be paid in full.

2. How useful is **Source B** as evidence of Mary's support for the Church of Scotland in 1566? 4

3. Describe the events which led to Mary, Queen of Scots being made a prisoner in Loch Leven Castle. 5

[END OF CONTEXT 3]

Marks

HISTORICAL STUDY: SCOTTISH AND BRITISH

CONTEXT 4: THE COMING OF THE CIVIL WAR, 1603–1642

Answer the following questions using recalled knowledge and information from the sources where appropriate.

Source A is part of Parliament's Petition of Right presented to the king in 1628.

Source A

> i) No man should be compelled to make any gift, loan, benevolence, tax or similar charge to the Crown without consent of Parliament.
> ii) No free man should be detained in prison without due cause shown.
> iii) Soldiers and sailors should not be billeted upon private citizens without their agreement.
> iv) There should be no martial law in time of peace.

1. How useful is **Source A** as evidence of the poor relations between Crown and Parliament in the reign of King Charles I? **4**

Source B is about Charles I's problems over religion in Scotland.

Source B

> In 1633 Charles came to Scotland to be crowned, accompanied by his new Archbishop of Canterbury. The coronation service was held in St Giles with candles, crucifix and full Anglican rites. Presbyterian ministers were ordered to wear Anglican surplices at services. The General Assembly had not met since 1618 and presbyteries were threatened with dissolution. Feelings were soon running high against the king.

2. Why did Charles I encounter difficulties with the Presbyterians in Scotland? (Use **Source B** and recall.) **5**

3. Describe the main activities of the Long Parliament against the king from 1640 until the outbreak of war in 1642. **5**

[END OF CONTEXT 4]

HISTORICAL STUDY: SCOTTISH AND BRITISH

CONTEXT 5: "ANE END OF ANE AULD SANG": SCOTLAND AND THE TREATY OF UNION, 1690s–1715

Answer the following questions using recalled knowledge and information from the sources where appropriate.

Source A is about Scottish opposition to the Act of Union.

Source A

> By an incorporating union, Scotland will become poorer than ever. Why so? Because Scotsmen will spend ten times more in England than they do now, and Scotland will run out of money. Scottish Members of Parliament will need money to live in London and Scottish noblemen will move there permanently as well. Some argue there would be advantages in trading with English colonies, but as I see it, English manufacturers will destroy our own industries.

1. Why did many Scots oppose the Union of 1707? (Use **Source A** and recall.)

Source B is from a letter written in 1707 by the Earl of Seafield who was a member of the Scottish government.

Source B

> It is impossible to state exactly how much was given to the Duke of Atholl, the Marquis of Tweeddale and the Earls of Roxburghe, Marchmont and Cromartie without revealing exactly how much has been given to everybody else. So far, this has been kept a secret and revealing this information at present would cause embarrassment.

2. How useful is **Source B** as evidence about how some Scottish nobles were persuaded to support the Act of Union?

3. Describe the events that led to the Jacobite Rising of 1715.

[END OF CONTEXT 5]

HISTORICAL STUDY: SCOTTISH AND BRITISH

CONTEXT 6: IMMIGRANTS AND EXILES: SCOTLAND, 1830s–1930s

Answer the following questions using recalled knowledge and information from the sources where appropriate.

Source A explains why Irish people came to Scotland.

Source A

> South-West areas of Scotland like Ayrshire were close to Ireland and so attracted Irish people to go there. A large number settled in the Glasgow area as many ships with cheap fares arrived there. During the year 1848 the number of people landing in Glasgow numbered a thousand a week. Many Irish people went to Dundee where they found work in the Dundee jute industry. Some Irish men and women came to Scotland for just part of the year and then returned home. They mainly worked on farms at times such as the harvest.

1. Why did many Irish people come to Scotland in the nineteenth century? (Use **Source A** and recall.) **5**

Source B is from a statement made by a cotton manufacturer in Glasgow in 1836.

Source B

> When the Irish first come over here, both the parents and the children are generally very decent and respectable. After they have been here some time their behaviour deteriorates. The change comes about by mixing with the lowest dregs of our Scottish working population.

2. How useful is **Source B** as evidence of Scottish attitudes to Irish immigrants in the 1830s? **4**

3. In what ways did Scottish immigrants help develop countries where they settled? **5**

[END OF CONTEXT 6]

HISTORICAL STUDY: SCOTTISH AND BRITISH

> CONTEXT 7(a): FROM THE CRADLE TO THE GRAVE? SOCIAL WELFARE IN BRITAIN, 1890s–1951

Answer the following questions using recalled knowledge and information from the sources where appropriate.

Source A is about conditions in London around 1890 by a campaigner against poverty.

Source A

> In one cellar a sanitary inspector reports finding a father, mother, three children and four pigs! In another room a missionary found a man ill with smallpox, his wife just recovering from the birth of her eighth child, and the children running about half naked and covered with dirt. Elsewhere was a poor widow, her three children, and a child who had been dead thirteen days.

1. How useful is **Source A** as evidence of the effects of poverty in Britain in the late nineteenth century? **4**

2. In what ways did the Second World War change people's attitude to poverty? **5**

Source B explains the effects of Labour welfare reforms.

Source B

> The National Insurance and National Assistance Acts meant everyone would be given help "from the cradle to the grave". The National Health Service Act of 1946 gave free medical care to all. All of these acts needed a lot of people to administer them. Some 200 000 homes a year were built between 1948 and 1951. The Labour government embarked on an ambitious school building programme.

3. Why were the Labour welfare reforms of 1945 to 1951 thought to be a great success? (Use **Source B** and recall.) **5**

[END OF CONTEXT 7(a)]

Marks

HISTORICAL STUDY: SCOTTISH AND BRITISH

CONTEXT 7(b): CAMPAIGNING FOR CHANGE: SOCIAL CHANGE IN SCOTLAND, 1900s–1979

Answer the following questions using recalled knowledge and information from the sources where appropriate.

Source A is about events on Clydeside in 1919.

Source A

> In the period just after the Great War there was a wave of working-class protest. It was feared that soldiers returning from war would find no work and many women had also lost their jobs. The government was worried that the workers of Clydeside would attempt to copy the Bolshevik revolution of 1917. There was a great deal of political unrest and some of the protesters even called for a Scottish Workers' Republic.

1. Why did some people fear that revolution was breaking out on Clydeside in 1919? (Use **Source A** and recall.) — 5

Source B is from an interview with a radio repairman in the 1930s.

Source B

> When a radio went wrong, it was like a death in the family. Sometimes when I arrived on the street a cheer went up and people would willingly pay whatever it took to get the set working again. It made me feel terribly important as I was treated with the same respect as a doctor.

2. How useful is **Source B** as evidence about the popularity of radio in the 1930s? — 4

3. Describe the changes that took place in industry in Scotland after 1945. — 5

[END OF CONTEXT 7(b)]

HISTORICAL STUDY: SCOTTISH AND BRITISH

CONTEXT 8: A TIME OF TROUBLES: IRELAND, 1900–1923

Answer the following questions using recalled knowledge and information from the sources where appropriate.

Source A explains why support for Sinn Fein increased in Ireland.

Source A

> In 1917 Sinn Fein won two by-elections. One of the men elected was Eamon De Valera. He had taken part in the Easter Rising but had avoided execution because he was born in America. De Valera took charge of Sinn Fein and reorganised it. Within the year all nationalist groups in Ireland had been united and Sinn Fein became the leading Irish party. As time went on the public began to see Sinn Fein as the main opposition to British rule.

1. Why did support for Sinn Fein increase in Ireland between 1916 and 1918? (Use **Source A** and recall.) 5

2. Describe the terms of the Anglo-Irish Treaty of 1921. 5

Source B is part of a letter from a District Police Inspector to the British Minister of Home Affairs in 1923.

Source B

> Some members of these Protestant groups are little better than hooligans. Their only aim is the extermination of Catholics by any and every means. They commit the deliberate and cold-blooded murder of harmless Catholics, shooting into Catholic houses and throwing bombs into Catholic areas. They have become as bad as the rebel gunmen. No-one obeys the law.

3. How useful is **Source B** as evidence of the violence in Ireland after partition? 4

[END OF CONTEXT 8]

[END OF PART 2: SCOTTISH AND BRITISH CONTEXTS]

PART 3:

HISTORICAL STUDY: EUROPEAN AND WORLD

CONTEXT 1: THE NORMAN CONQUEST, 1060–1153

Answer the following questions using recalled knowledge and information from the sources where appropriate.

Source A is about the Battle of Hastings.

Source A

> Harold greatly weakened his chances of success through his rashness in moving south to meet William before he could gather together all the men available to him. Despite this, the Normans found it difficult to break through the ranks of the English forces. They gained the upper hand only when the defenders broke their own battle-line to pursue Normans they mistakenly thought were retreating.

Marks

1. Why did King Harold lose the Battle of Hastings? (Use **Source A** and recall.) **5**

2. Describe William I's methods of controlling England after 1066. **5**

Source B is about the role of castles in the Norman Conquest. It was written by the medieval chronicler Orderic Vitalis.

Source B

> The fortifications which the Normans called castles were hardly known in England. In spite of their courage and love of fighting, this meant the English could only put up a weak show of resistance. Certainly in King William's time men suffered great oppression and much injustice because he ordered castles to be built which were a sore burden on the poor.

Source C is about castles in the Norman Conquest. It was written by the modern historian M Morris in 2003.

Source C

> Recently historians have begun to suggest the importance of castles has been exaggerated. New technical ideas such as the building of castles made little difference between the Normans and the English. Knocking out the Anglo-Saxons in battle was the key thing. Erecting huge mounds of earth with castles on them was all very well, but in fact, they were really only symbols of lordship and not weapons of conquest.

3. Compare the views of **Sources B** and **C** on the role of castles in the Norman Conquest. **4**

[END OF CONTEXT 1]

HISTORICAL STUDY: EUROPEAN AND WORLD

CONTEXT 2: THE CROSS AND THE CRESCENT: THE FIRST CRUSADE, 1096–1125

Answer the following questions using recalled knowledge and information from the sources where appropriate.

Source A explains why people joined the First Crusade.

Source A

> After Pope Urban's speech many people set off on Crusade. Some went because they said they wanted to serve God. Others went because they believed it was their duty to help the Christians in the east. For some, their reasons for going were far more practical. Famine and plague had terrified people to the point where they were desperate to leave Europe. Recapturing Jerusalem seemed an attractive idea.

1. Why did people join the First Crusade? (Use **Source A** and recall.) 5

Source B describes the relationship between the Emperor Alexius and Bohemond. It was written in 1096 by a Crusader who travelled with Bohemond.

Source B

> When Alexius heard that the honourable knight Bohemond had arrived at Constantinople, he immediately began to panic. Alexius was so afraid of him that he began to think of ways to trick and to get rid of Bohemond. Only by God's will did his tricks fail. When he finally met Bohemond, Alexius insisted that he take an oath of loyalty. The emperor did this because he feared the power Bohemond had over the other knights.

Source B describes the relationship between the Emperor Alexius and Bohemond. It was written by Alexius's daughter, Anna.

Source C

> Bohemond is the most dishonest and dishonourable man I have ever met. The minute he arrived in Constantinople it was obvious that he wanted to steal Alexius's land. Alexius, knowing what kind of man Bohemond was, insisted that he take an oath of loyalty. The emperor did this because he did not trust Bohemond. This cunning tactic spoiled any of Bohemond's plans to trick Alexius and take his land.

2. Compare **Sources B** and **C** as views of the relationship between Alexius and Bohemond. 4

3. Describe the problems faced by the Crusaders after the capture of Jerusalem. 5

[END OF CONTEXT 2]

Marks

HISTORICAL STUDY: EUROPEAN AND WORLD

CONTEXT 3: WAR, DEATH AND REVOLT IN MEDIEVAL EUROPE, 1328–1436

Answer the following questions using recalled knowledge and information from the sources where appropriate.

Source A is about the growing tension between England and France in 1337.

Source A

> English monarchs still had some lands in France and Edward III was looking to extend his kingdom. Also Edward's mother was a French princess which allowed him to claim that he was the rightful King of France. The French argued that no woman could have any claim to the French throne. Edward started to make preparations for war. His people were anxious to support him. They were annoyed by the way the French had stopped Flemish merchants from buying English wool.

1. Why was England preparing for war with France by 1337? (Use **Source A** and recall.) **5**

Sources B and **C** describe the effects of the Black Death on England.

Source B

> Sheep and oxen strayed through the fields and among the crops and there was no-one to drive them off or collect them. Livestock perished in great numbers throughout all districts due to a lack of shepherds and other farm workers. In the autumn no-one could be hired for less than 4 pennies plus meals. For this reason crops perished but in the year of the plague there was so much corn it did not matter.

Source C

> There was a shortage of labour because so many people, particularly peasants, died of the disease. Many farm animals also died. Lords, who relied on their peasants to farm their land, became desperate. They were forced to pay more to each peasant worker. Wages rose so much that Edward III had to issue new coins called groats and half groats (a groat was worth 4 pennies).

2. How far do **Sources B** and **C** agree about the effects of the Black Death on England? **4**

3. Describe Henry V's campaign in France between 1415 and 1420. **5**

[*END OF CONTEXT 3*]

HISTORICAL STUDY: EUROPEAN AND WORLD

CONTEXT 4: NEW WORLDS: EUROPE IN THE AGE OF EXPANSION, 1480s–1530s

Answer the following questions using recalled knowledge and information from the sources where appropriate.

1. Describe Columbus's first voyage to the New World in 1492. **5**

Source A is from a letter written by the fifteenth-century Italian map-maker Paul Toscanelli to Christopher Columbus.

Source A

> Paul, the scholar and physician, to Christopher Columbus greetings.
> I understand your magnificent and great desire to explore and find a way to where the spices grow. I therefore send you a map made by my own hands, on which are drawn the coasts and islands from which you must begin to make your journey westwards and the places at which you should arrive.

Source B is part of a letter by the King of Spain in support of the voyage of the explorer Ferdinand Magellan in the early sixteenth century.

Source B

> According to the information and maps I have obtained from persons who have seen them, I know for certain that there are spices in the islands of the Moluccas. You are ordered to seek them with this fleet. I command that in every matter of navigation you follow the decisions of the bearer of this letter, Ferdinand Magellan, whose greatest desire is to undertake this voyage to discover new lands.

2. Compare **Sources A** and **B** as views of why voyages of exploration took place between the 1480s and 1530s. **4**

In **Source C** a Conquistador describes a battle between the native peoples of the New World and their Spanish conquerors.

Source C

> The steady firing of our artillery and musketeers did the enemy much damage. Those who came too close to us were soon forced back by the sword-play of our men. Our horsemen were so skilful and fought so bravely that, after God who showered His blessings upon us, they were our greatest asset. However so many of the enemy charged upon us that only by a miracle of sword-play could we make them give way and maintain our battle formation.

3. Why were the native peoples of the New World unable to defeat the Spanish Conquistadors? (Use **Source C** and recall.) **5**

[END OF CONTEXT 4]

HISTORICAL STUDY: EUROPEAN AND WORLD

CONTEXT 5: "TEA AND FREEDOM": THE AMERICAN REVOLUTION, 1763–1783

Answer the following questions using recalled knowledge and information from the sources where appropriate.

1. Describe the events in Boston in 1770 which became known as the "Boston Massacre". **5**

Source A was written by George III in 1776 defending British rule in the American colonies.

Source A

> I believe the spirit of the British nation too great and the resources with which God has blessed her too numerous, to give up so many colonies which she has established with great care. We have helped these colonies grow and become successful. We have protected and defended them at the expense of much blood and at great cost to us.

Source B was written by Thomas Paine in 1776 criticising Britain's rule in the American colonies.

Source B

> America would have flourished as much and probably more, even if no European nation had taken notice of her. America is so rich because of her trade in essential goods which will always be needed by other countries. Britain has defended the American continent at not only her own expense but also at the expense of the colonists. This she has done not out of concern but for trade and power.

2. Compare the views expressed in **Sources A** and **B** about British rule in the American colonies. **4**

Source C explains the importance of French support for the colonists.

Source C

> After the American victory at Saratoga in 1778, France officially entered the war on the American side. The French wanted to avenge their defeat in 1763. From the beginning the French secretly lent the American government money to keep the war going. At the battle of Yorktown the majority of Washington's army was equipped and supplied by the French. Indeed the majority of the 15 000 soldiers were French. The French navy also trapped Cornwallis's soldiers in Yorktown.

3. Why was French support important to the colonists throughout the Revolutionary War? (Use **Source C** and recall.) **5**

[END OF CONTEXT 5]

HISTORICAL STUDY: EUROPEAN AND WORLD

CONTEXT 6: "THIS ACCURSED TRADE": THE BRITISH SLAVE TRADE AND ITS ABOLITION, 1770–1807

Answer the following questions using recalled knowledge and information from the sources where appropriate.

1. Describe the ways Britain profited from the slave trade. **5**

Sources A and **B** describe the effects of the Atlantic slave trade on Africa and its peoples.

Source A

> Nowhere in history have a people experienced such a terrible ordeal as Africans during the Atlantic slave trade. Over nearly four centuries of the trade, millions of healthy men, women and children were savagely torn from their homeland, herded into ships, and dispersed all over the so called New World. Although there is no way to work out exactly how many people perished, it has been estimated that about 10 million Africans survived the Middle Passage.

Source B

> The Atlantic slave trade spelled disaster for Africa and its peoples. For four hundred years, millions of the healthiest young people of the region were stolen from their homeland. No-one is sure exactly how many were sold into slavery but probably about 11 million African people arrived in the New World between 1450 and 1850. Add to that the number who died in war or on the journey and you can begin to see the devastating effect on families at that time.

2. How far do **Sources A** and **B** agree about the effects of the slave trade on Africa and its peoples? **4**

Source C explains why it took so long to abolish the slave trade.

Source C

> The supporters of the slave trade were well organised and influential. Although Wilberforce introduced his first bill to abolish it in 1789, it took a full eighteen years to end the evil. Plantation owners were often Members of Parliament who also had the support of George III. As a result, they created many difficulties for the abolitionists.

3. Why did it take so long to persuade parliament to abolish the slave trade? (Use **Source C** and recall.) **5**

[END OF CONTEXT 6]

HISTORICAL STUDY: EUROPEAN AND WORLD

CONTEXT 7: CITIZENS! THE FRENCH REVOLUTION, 1789–1794

Answer the following questions using recalled knowledge and information from the sources where appropriate.

1. Describe the difficulties faced by Louis XVI's government by 1789. **5**

Source A is from a list of complaints sent to the Estates General from a village in the south of France, 1789.

Source A

> We are heavily burdened by feudal dues even though our soil is barren. When our rents and taxes have been paid, we have hardly a penny left. The landlords grow fat from our labours yet pay no taxes. We pay, indeed, without understanding what we are paying for. There is only one thing that we ask of the Estates General – to find a way to relieve our poverty.

Source B is from a list of complaints from a village in the west of France, 1789.

Source B

> We most humbly ask that all citizens, no matter who they are, contribute to all the taxes according to their income. We should be told who takes a share of the taxes – for example, how much goes to the army. Bear in mind that the land grows every day more unproductive and that our burdens should be lightened.

2. How far do **Sources A** and **B** agree about the complaints of French peasants before the Revolution? **4**

Source C explains the feelings of many French people in 1791.

Source C

> The Third Estate had fought together against the privileges of the Church, nobility and monarchy yet it had become increasingly clear that the revolution was fast becoming a victory for the middle class. The aristocracy were to be given compensation for the loss of their feudal rights. Lands taken away from the Church were sold in such a way that poorer peasants could not afford to buy them. Workshops for the unemployed were closed down.

3. Why were many French people disappointed in the revolution by 1791? (Use **Source C** and recall.) **5**

[END OF CONTEXT 7]

HISTORICAL STUDY: EUROPEAN AND WORLD

CONTEXT 8: CAVOUR, GARIBALDI AND THE MAKING OF ITALY, 1815–1870

Answer the following questions using recalled knowledge and information from the sources where appropriate.

In **Sources A** and **B** two historians discuss the effects of the Crimean War.

Source A

> Piedmont's participation in the Crimean War had been unpopular and unproductive. However, the war did change the international situation in Piedmont's favour. Austria's hesitant approach to the war meant that she lost the friendship of Russia. This left her isolated. Her failure to support Britain and France meant she could not expect help from these two great powers when it came to controlling the Italian states. Austria's isolation would prove crucial in helping to bring about Italian unification.

Source B

> The Crimean War was a critical turning point for the cause of Italian unification. Austria was now isolated diplomatically. She had lost her great ally, Russia, and was forced to ally with unreliable Prussia. Neither France nor Britain would be sympathetic to maintaining Austrian power in northern Italy and its dominant position over the whole peninsula. Piedmont's participation in the Crimean War also confirmed her position as the leading state in Italy.

1. To what extent do **Sources A** and **B** agree about the effects of the Crimean War on Austria's diplomatic position? **4**

In **Source C** a journalist from the time describes Mazzini's role in Italian unification.

> Guiseppe Mazzini did more than anyone to publicise the great aim of Italian unity. He was an active member of the Carbonari but when it became clear to him that its badly organised conspiracies were making no progress he founded a national movement called Young Italy. He was sentenced to death for his activities and spent most of his life in exile hatching plots against the rulers of the Italian states.

2. Why was Guiseppe Mazzini important to Italian unification? (Use **Source C** and recall.) **5**

3. Describe the contribution of Guiseppe Garibaldi to Italian unification. **5**

[END OF CONTEXT 8]

HISTORICAL STUDY: EUROPEAN AND WORLD

CONTEXT 9: IRON AND BLOOD? BISMARCK AND THE CREATION OF THE GERMAN EMPIRE, 1815–1871

Answer the following questions using recalled knowledge and information from the sources where appropriate.

1. Describe the events of the 1848 Revolution in Germany. **5**

In **Source A** the Prussian Field Marshal, von Moltke, describes Prussia's preparations for the war against Austria in 1866.

Source A

> Our leaders prepared carefully for the war with Austria. We ensured the support of other countries. They did not wish to increase the size of Prussia but wanted to increase our influence. Austria had to give up her control over the German states but not a bit of territory was to be taken from her. Austria had exhausted her strength. Prussia felt it was her duty to assume the leadership of the German races and now felt strong enough to do so.

In **Source B** a modern historian describes the preparations of Prussia for the war against Austria in 1866.

Source B

> In preparation for the war against Austria, Bismarck's leadership was crucial. He secured the neutrality of Napoleon III and made an alliance with Italy to attack Austria in the rear if war should come. Bismarck insisted that not a bit of Austrian territory should be annexed by Prussia. The object was to ensure the supremacy of Prussia over the north German states.

2. How far do **Sources A** and **B** agree about Prussia's preparations for the war against Austria in 1866? **4**

Source C explains the growing hostility between Prussia and France from 1868 to 1870.

Source C

> In 1868 the new government of Spain began to look for a new monarch. They approached Prince Leopold of Hohenzollern. This was opposed by France since having a German as king in Spain would alter the balance of power against France. The news of the Hohenzollern candidature caused a hostile reaction in Paris. The French government demanded the King of Prussia's guarantee that the Hohenzollerns would never claim the Spanish throne. At Ems, the king politely refused to give any such guarantee.

3. Why was there growing hostility between Prussia and France between 1868 and 1870? (Use **Source C** and recall.) **5**

[END OF CONTEXT 9]

HISTORICAL STUDY: EUROPEAN AND WORLD

CONTEXT 10: THE RED FLAG: LENIN AND THE RUSSIAN REVOLUTION, 1894–1921

Answer the following questions using recalled knowledge and information from the sources where appropriate.

1. What methods did the Tsar use to maintain his control over Russia before 1914? **5**

Source A is part of a letter from the Tsarina to the Tsar describing the situation in Petrograd in February 1917.

Source A

> The trouble comes from a few idlers, well-dressed people, wounded soldiers and school girls. We hear of students coming into town and telling people to stay off the streets in the morning or they could be shot. What lies! Of course the cab-drivers and motormen are now on strike. But it is all different from 1905. The people all worship you and only want bread.

Source B is part of a letter from the President of the Duma to the Tsar. It also describes the situation in Petrograd in February 1917.

Source B

> The situation is serious. Petrograd is in a state of chaos. The government is paralysed; the transport system has broken down so supplies of fuel are completely disorganised. Discontent is general and on the increase. There is wild shooting in the streets. It is urgent that someone whom the people trust should form a new government.

2. How far do **Sources A** and **B** disagree about the unrest in Petrograd in February 1917? **4**

In **Source C** Trotsky explains why the Red Army was victorious in the Civil War.

Source C

> A flabby, panicky mob could be transformed in two or three weeks into an efficient fighting force. What was needed for this? It needed a few dozen good commanders who were experienced fighters. Communists ready to make any sacrifice for the revolution were essential. Supplies such as boots for the barefooted, underwear, food, tobacco and matches attracted new recruits who were also encouraged by an energetic propaganda campaign.

3. Why was the Red Army victorious in the Civil War? (Use **Source C** and recall.) **5**

[END OF CONTEXT 10]

HISTORICAL STUDY: EUROPEAN AND WORLD

CONTEXT 11: FREE AT LAST? RACE RELATIONS IN THE USA, 1918–1968

Answer the following questions using recalled knowledge and information from the sources where appropriate.

Source A is by a Senator from Alabama in 1921. He is explaining why he wanted immigration controls.

Source A

> As soon as the immigrants step off the decks of their ships our problem has begun – Bolshevism, red anarchy, crooks and kidnappers. Thousands come here who never take the oath to support our Constitution and to become citizens of the United States. They do not respect what our flag represents. They pay allegiance to some other country and flag while they live upon the benefits of our own. They are of no service whatever to our people. They constitute a menace and a danger to us every day.

Source B is a description by Robert Coughlan of the growth of support for the Ku Klux Klan in the 1920s.

Source B

> It may be asked why, then, did the town take so enthusiastically to the Klan? Many old stock Americans believed they were in danger of being overrun. The "foreigners were ruining our country"; and so anything "foreign" was "un-American" and a menace. Cars were draped with the American flag and some carried homemade signs with Klan slogans such as "America for the Americans".

1. How far do **Sources A** and **B** agree about American attitudes to immigrants in the 1920s? **4**

2. Describe the events of the Montgomery bus boycott. **5**

Source C explains why the Black Panthers gained support.

Source C

> The leaders of the Black Panthers argued that black Americans were victims of white aggression and it was now time to defend black Americans. When Huey Newton said things like "The police have never been our protectors", the big newspapers gave the Panthers a negative image. Journalists did not publicise the self-help programmes organised by the Black Panthers, who also had a ten-point programme. This included demands for freedom and the release of all black people held in prisons.

3. Why did the Black Panthers gain support from many black Americans? (Use **Source C** and recall.) **5**

[END OF CONTEXT 11]

HISTORICAL STUDY: EUROPEAN AND WORLD

CONTEXT 12: THE ROAD TO WAR, 1933–1939

Answer the following questions using recalled knowledge and information from the sources where appropriate.

Source A is about the reoccupation of the Rhineland, 1936.

Source A

> Germany was able to score an important victory without having to fire a shot. Hitler knew that his strategy had required taking a great risk because France was much stronger. After he had shown strong leadership Hitler was treated with greater respect abroad. France's allies in Eastern Europe began to see Germany as the stronger nation while in the west the Belgians moved towards a position of neutrality instead of supporting France.

1. Why was the reoccupation of the Rhineland in 1936 important for Hitler? (Use **Source A** and recall.) **5**

2. Describe the events of the Czechoslovakian crisis of 1938 that led to the Munich Settlement. **5**

In **Sources B** and **C** two modern historians give their views on appeasement.

Source B

> Appeasement was a practical solution to make peace and settle disputes with Germany. This approach was adopted because it was believed that Germany had been treated unfairly at Versailles. For the British and French leaders it was not a policy of cowardice or weakness in the face of threats. Instead, it was a policy of preventing war in the belief that Europe could not survive a bloodbath such as the Great War.

Source C

> Appeasement often meant a surrender of principles. Chamberlain's approach to appeasement was based on the belief that Nazism, horrible as it was, was here to stay and Britain ought to deal with it. Under his direction it became a policy of cowardice and dishonour – a way of gaining short-term peace at someone else's expense.

3. How far do **Sources B** and **C** disagree about the policy of appeasement? **4**

[END OF CONTEXT 12]

Marks

HISTORICAL STUDY: EUROPEAN AND WORLD

CONTEXT 13: IN THE SHADOW OF THE BOMB: THE COLD WAR, 1945–1985

Answer the following questions using recalled knowledge and information from the sources where appropriate.

1. What was meant by "the Cold War"?   **5**

Source A is from the speech by President Kennedy on television to the American people, 22 October 1962.

Source A

> To halt this build up, a strict quarantine of all offensive military equipment being shipped to Cuba is being introduced. All ships of any kind bound for Cuba from whatever nation or port will, if found to contain cargoes of offensive weapons, be turned back. We are not at this time, however, denying the necessities of life as the Soviets attempted to do in their Berlin blockade of 1948.

Source B is from the letter sent by Nikita Khrushchev to President Kennedy, 24 October 1962.

Source B

> You, Mr President, are not declaring quarantine, but rather an ultimatum, and you are threatening that if we do not obey your orders, you will use force to turn back the ships. Think about what you are saying! And you want to persuade me to agree to this! What does it mean to agree to these demands? It would mean for us to conduct our relations with other countries not by reason, but by yielding to tyranny. You are not appealing to reason; you want to intimidate us.

2. Compare the views in **Sources A** and **B** on the Cuban Missile Crisis.   **4**

Source C explains why there was a thaw in the Cold War in the late 1960s.

Source C

> The tensions of the 1960s, which had brought them to the brink of nuclear war, caused the superpowers to rethink their plans. This led to a thaw in the Cold War. Both sides had important reasons to seek a relaxation in tensions. Leonid Brezhnev and the rest of the Soviet leadership felt the economic burden of the nuclear arms race was too great. The American economy was also in financial trouble as a result of the Vietnam War. Johnson, and to a lesser extent Nixon, were having difficulty funding the government welfare programme.

3. Why did both sides want détente by the late 1960s? (Use **Source C** and recall.)   **5**

[END OF CONTEXT 13]

[END OF PART 3: EUROPEAN AND WORLD CONTEXTS]

[END OF QUESTION PAPER]

[BLANK PAGE]

INTERMEDIATE 2
2008

[BLANK PAGE]

X044/201

NATIONAL
QUALIFICATIONS
2008

MONDAY, 26 MAY
9.00 AM – 10.45 AM

HISTORY
INTERMEDIATE 2

The instructions for this paper are on *Page two*. Read them carefully before you begin your answers.

Some sources in this examination have been adapted or translated.

INSTRUCTIONS

Answer **one** question from Part 1, The Short Essay

Answer **one** context from Part 2, Scottish and British

Answer **one** context from Part 3, European and World

Answer **one** other context from

    either Part 2, Scottish and British

    or   Part 3, European and World

Contents

Part 1 Short Essay Questions.
Answer **one** question only.   Pages 4–6

Part 2 Scottish and British Contexts

1. Murder in the Cathedral: Crown, Church and People, 1154–1173   Page 8
2. Wallace, Bruce and the Wars of Independence, 1286–1328   Page 9
3. Mary, Queen of Scots and the Scottish Reformation, 1540s–1587   Page 10
4. The Coming of the Civil War, 1603–1642   Page 11
5. "Ane End of Ane Auld Sang": Scotland and the Treaty of Union, 1690s–1715   Page 12
6. Immigrants and Exiles: Scotland, 1830s–1930s   Page 13
7.(a) From the Cradle to the Grave? Social Welfare in Britain, 1890s–1951   Page 14

OR

7.(b) Campaigning for Change: Social Change in Scotland, 1900s–1979   Page 15
8. A Time of Troubles: Ireland, 1900–1923   Page 16

Part 3 European and World Contexts

1. The Norman Conquest, 1060–1153   Page 17
2. The Cross and the Crescent: The First Crusade, 1096–1125   Page 18
3. War, Death and Revolt in Medieval Europe, 1328–1436   Page 19
4. New Worlds: Europe in the Age of Expansion, 1480s–1530s   Page 20
5. "Tea and Freedom": The American Revolution, 1763–1783   Page 21
6. "This Accursed Trade": The British Slave Trade and its Abolition, 1770–1807   Page 22
7. Citizens! The French Revolution, 1789–1794   Page 23
8. Cavour, Garibaldi and the Making of Italy, 1815–1870   Page 24
9. Iron and Blood? Bismarck and the Creation of the German Empire, 1815–1871   Page 25
10. The Red Flag: Lenin and the Russian Revolution, 1894–1921   Page 26
11. Free at Last? Race Relations in the USA, 1918–1968   Page 27
12. The Road to War, 1933–1939   Page 28
13. In the Shadow of the Bomb: The Cold War, 1945–1985   Page 29

[Turn over

PART 1: THE SHORT ESSAY

Answer **one** question. For this question you should write a short essay using your own knowledge. The essay should include an introduction, development and conclusion. Each question is worth 8 marks.

SCOTTISH AND BRITISH CONTEXTS:

CONTEXT 1: MURDER IN THE CATHEDRAL: CROWN, CHURCH AND PEOPLE, 1154–1173

Question 1: Explain why the Church was important in the Middle Ages.   8

CONTEXT 2: WALLACE, BRUCE AND THE WARS OF INDEPENDENCE, 1286–1328

Question 2: Explain why there was a succession problem in Scotland between 1286 and 1292.   8

CONTEXT 3: MARY, QUEEN OF SCOTS AND THE SCOTTISH REFORMATION, 1540s–1587

Question 3: Explain why her marriage to Darnley caused problems for Mary, Queen of Scots.   8

CONTEXT 4: THE COMING OF THE CIVIL WAR, 1603–1642

Question 4: Explain why Charles I declared war on Parliament in 1642.   8

CONTEXT 5: "ANE END OF ANE AULD SANG": SCOTLAND AND THE TREATY OF UNION, 1690s–1715

Question 5: Explain why some Scots thought a Union with England would make Scotland richer.   8

CONTEXT 6: IMMIGRANTS AND EXILES: SCOTLAND, 1830s–1930s

Question 6: Explain why many Scots resented immigrants from Ireland in the nineteenth century.   8

CONTEXT 7(a): FROM THE CRADLE TO THE GRAVE? SOCIAL WELFARE IN BRITAIN, 1890s–1951

Question 7(a): Explain why the Labour welfare reforms after 1945 were successful in meeting the needs of the people.   8

Marks

CONTEXT 7(b): CAMPAIGNING FOR CHANGE: SOCIAL CHANGE IN SCOTLAND, 1900s–1979

Question 7(b): Explain why many Scottish women were able to lead better lives in the period 1918–1939. **8**

CONTEXT 8: A TIME OF TROUBLES: IRELAND, 1900–1923

Question 8: Explain why the Easter Rising of 1916 failed. **8**

EUROPEAN AND WORLD CONTEXTS:

CONTEXT 1: THE NORMAN CONQUEST, 1060–1153

Question 9: Explain why Anglo-Saxon opposition to William was ineffective after 1066. **8**

CONTEXT 2: THE CROSS AND THE CRESCENT: THE FIRST CRUSADE, 1096–1125

Question 10: Explain why the First Crusade was able to achieve its aims. **8**

CONTEXT 3: WAR, DEATH AND REVOLT IN MEDIEVAL EUROPE, 1328–1436

Question 11: Explain why the French were eventually successful in the Hundred Years' War. **8**

CONTEXT 4: NEW WORLDS: EUROPE IN THE AGE OF EXPANSION, 1480s–1530s

Question 12: Explain why developments in technology were important in encouraging voyages of exploration. **8**

CONTEXT 5: "TEA AND FREEDOM": THE AMERICAN REVOLUTION, 1763–1783

Question 13: Explain why some American colonists remained loyal to Britain. **8**

CONTEXT 6: "THIS ACCURSED TRADE": THE BRITISH SLAVE TRADE AND ITS ABOLITION, 1770–1807

Question 14: Explain why many people were in favour of the Slave Trade in the eighteenth century. **8**

[Turn over

CONTEXT 7: CITIZENS! THE FRENCH REVOLUTION, 1789–1794

Question 15: Explain why France became a republic in 1792. **8**

CONTEXT 8: CAVOUR, GARIBALDI AND THE MAKING OF ITALY, 1815–1870

Question 16: Explain why Italy became a unified country by 1870. **8**

CONTEXT 9: IRON AND BLOOD? BISMARCK AND THE CREATION OF THE GERMAN EMPIRE, 1815–1871

Question 17: Explain why Prussia succeeded in uniting Germany by 1871. **8**

CONTEXT 10: THE RED FLAG: LENIN AND THE RUSSIAN REVOLUTION, 1894–1921

Question 18: Explain why there was discontent among Russian industrial workers in the years leading up to 1914. **8**

CONTEXT 11: FREE AT LAST? RACE RELATIONS IN THE USA, 1918–1968

Question 19: Explain why the Ku Klux Klan was feared in the 1920s and 1930s. **8**

CONTEXT 12: THE ROAD TO WAR, 1933–1939

Question 20: Explain why Britain allowed Germany to ignore the Treaty of Versailles during the 1930s. **8**

CONTEXT 13: IN THE SHADOW OF THE BOMB: THE COLD WAR, 1945–1985

Question 21: Explain why a Cold War developed after the Second World War. **8**

[END OF PART 1: THE SHORT ESSAY]

[Turn over for PART 2: SCOTTISH AND BRITISH CONTEXTS on *Page eight*

PART 2:

HISTORICAL STUDY: SCOTTISH AND BRITISH

CONTEXT 1: MURDER IN THE CATHEDRAL: CROWN, CHURCH AND PEOPLE, 1154–1173

Answer the following questions using recalled knowledge and information from the sources where appropriate.

Source A explains why Henry II was forced to increase his power when he became king in 1154.

Source A

> Henry's first task was to destroy all the castles that had been built without the king's permission. Nineteen years of civil war had increased the power of the barons and reduced the authority of the king. Within three weeks of becoming king, Henry marched on Scarborough castle and defeated the Earl of York. Soon after, Henry dealt with the sheriffs who were deciding the law in their own areas. They were also corrupt and could no longer be trusted.

1. Why was Henry II forced to increase his power when he became king in 1154? (Use **Source A** and recall.) **5**

2. Describe the role of a knight in medieval society. **5**

Sources B and **C** describe the quarrel between Henry II and Archbishop Becket.

Source B

> It was the king's wish that members of the clergy who committed crimes be tried in the king's court and not in the Church court. Becket completely refused to agree to this. He argued that only God and not the king had the right to judge the clergy. Henry felt betrayed by Becket's defence of the Church. He immediately threatened Becket with exile and death.

Source C

> Becket's actions angered the king. Henry expected Becket to support him and not the Church. To his amazement Becket would not agree to the clergy being tried in the king's court. Henry threatened and bullied Becket but this did not work. Becket argued that the king received his power from God and therefore had no authority to judge clergymen.

3. How far do **Sources B** and **C** agree about the quarrel between Henry II and Archbishop Becket? **4**

[END OF CONTEXT 1]

Marks

HISTORICAL STUDY: SCOTTISH AND BRITISH

CONTEXT 2: WALLACE, BRUCE AND THE WARS OF INDEPENDENCE, 1286–1328

Answer the following questions using recalled knowledge and information from the sources where appropriate.

1. Describe what happened when Edward I attacked Berwick in 1296. **5**

Sources A and **B** describe the meeting of Bruce and the Red Comyn in 1306.

Source A

> While they were speaking, Bruce suddenly accused Comyn of betraying him. Comyn denied this. Just as he had planned, Bruce hit Comyn with a sword and left. When some evil folk told Bruce that Comyn would live, he ordered them to kill him beside the high altar.

Source B

> When Bruce accused Comyn of telling King Edward about him, Comyn said this was a lie. This evil speaker was then stabbed and wounded. Later, the monks laid Comyn beside the altar but, when he said that he thought he would live, his enemies hit him again. Thus he was taken away from this world.

2. How far do **Sources A** and **B** agree about what happened when Bruce and the Red Comyn met at Greyfriars Kirk in 1306? **4**

Source C is about the Battle of Bannockburn.

Source C

> Bruce's careful preparations for battle were ruined when Edward II moved his army to attack from the east and not from the south. However, this gave the much larger English army no room to move because they were surrounded by marshes and streams. Bruce decided to take advantage of this mistake and to attack them. The English were so jammed together and so tangled up that their leaders struggled to organise any defence and they lost all confidence in Edward II for leading them into this trap.

3. Why did the Scots win the Battle of Bannockburn? (Use **Source C** and recall.) **5**

[END OF CONTEXT 2]

HISTORICAL STUDY: SCOTTISH AND BRITISH

CONTEXT 3: MARY, QUEEN OF SCOTS AND THE SCOTTISH REFORMATION, 1540s–1587

Answer the following questions using recalled knowledge and information from the sources where appropriate.

1. Describe the events which forced Mary, Queen of Scots to leave Scotland in 1548. **5**

Source A is about the unpopularity of Riccio, Mary's secretary.

Source A

> Riccio had arrived in Scotland as a musician but he won the attention and friendship of Mary who made him a secretary. Darnley blamed Riccio for Mary's refusal to make him king. He also grew jealous of Mary's friendship with Riccio whose lively and witty company she enjoyed. Many of the Scottish nobles detested this low born Italian and believed him to be a secret agent of the Pope.

2. Why did many Scots dislike Riccio? (Use **Source A** and recall.) **5**

Sources B and **C** describe Mary's return to Edinburgh after her capture at Carberry, 1567.

Source B

> To her horror, Mary was placed under the guard of two very wicked young men. Dirty and so exhausted and faint, Mary was escorted back to Edinburgh. As she rode through the streets of Edinburgh, people shouted abuse at her, calling her a murderess and screaming "Burn her! Drown her!". By now, Mary was weeping.

Source C

> As she rode through the streets of Edinburgh the people shouted "Burn her! Kill her! Drown her! She is not fit to live." Two evil young thugs were guarding her and they joined in insulting her. Amazed, almost stunned, the Queen allowed tears of shock and humiliation to pour down her cheeks.

3. How far do **Sources B** and **C** agree about what happened to Mary after her capture at Carberry in 1567? **4**

[END OF CONTEXT 3]

HISTORICAL STUDY: SCOTTISH AND BRITISH

CONTEXT 4: THE COMING OF THE CIVIL WAR, 1603–1642

Answer the following questions using recalled knowledge and information from the sources where appropriate.

Sources A and **B** describe the attitude of the Stuarts to Scotland after the Union of the Crowns.

Source A

> After 1603 the Stuarts lost interest in Scotland and were really only concerned with England, which was the richer and more powerful kingdom. Scotland was governed like a distant province. The Stuarts only cared about Scotland when they needed men and money for their armies. From James VI onwards, they were glad to escape from a country with its troublesome Presbyterians.

Source B

> Scotland and England were much closer in size and wealth in the 1600s, so it's not true to say that Scotland was neglected because England was richer. The Stuarts remained vitally interested in Scottish affairs as Scotland was their original power base. The Stuarts were especially keen to impose their views on the Church as they saw the Presbyterians as a threat to their authority.

1. How far do **Sources A** and **B** agree about the attitude of the Stuarts to Scotland? **4**

Source C explains why James VI and I was unpopular with the English Parliament.

> The new king lost respect by giving money and power to his favourites at court. His coronation cost £20,000 and he spent lavishly on hunting and banquets. By 1610 he was seriously short of money. He increased his income by raising the customs duties on imported goods. The Members of Parliament argued that the king could not raise taxes without their permission. The sale of monopolies also brought in a great deal of money but made Parliament angry.

2. Why was James VI and I unpopular with the English Parliament between 1603 and 1625? (Use **Source C** and recall.) **5**

3. Describe the ways the Scots opposed Charles I over religion between 1637 and 1640. **5**

[END OF CONTEXT 4]

HISTORICAL STUDY: SCOTTISH AND BRITISH

CONTEXT 5: "ANE END OF ANE AULD SANG": SCOTLAND AND THE TREATY OF UNION, 1690s–1715

Answer the following questions using recalled knowledge and information from the sources where appropriate.

1. Describe the events leading up to the execution of Captain Green of the Worcester in 1705. **5**

Source A is about why Queen Anne wanted a Union between Scotland and England.

Source A

> Union was the solution favoured by Queen Anne and by Lord Godolphin. She found it difficult to govern Scotland from Westminster. Union would avoid any arguments about the succession because Anne was determined to secure the Protestant Succession. She also thought that the Union of the two countries would create a more powerful state. Besides, Union would protect England from any French threat in the future if the discontented Scots ever wanted to revive the Auld Alliance.

2. Why did Queen Anne want a Union between England and Scotland? (Use **Source A** and recall.) **5**

Sources B and **C** describe Scottish reaction to the Union between 1707 and 1714.

Source B

> The Scots soon became disillusioned with the Union because it did not bring immediate prosperity. The Church of Scotland was outraged when patronage was reintroduced to the Church of Scotland and Episcopalians were to be tolerated. The Malt Tax was introduced and many were angry as this broke the Treaty. It appeared to many Scots that politicians in London had the power to re-write the Treaty.

Source C

> For most people, life in most matters was unchanged but some were soon disappointed. Within a few years significant changes were made which they thought broke the terms of the Treaty of Union. Church Patronage obviously broke the Church of Scotland's Act of Security and angered its ministers. Many Scots were unhappy with the introduction of the Malt Tax as this could have had serious consequences.

3. How far do **Sources B** and **C** agree about the reasons for Scottish anger after the Union? **4**

[END OF CONTEXT 5]

HISTORICAL STUDY: SCOTTISH AND BRITISH

CONTEXT 6: IMMIGRANTS AND EXILES: SCOTLAND, 1830s–1930s

Answer the following questions using recalled knowledge and information from the sources where appropriate.

Sources A and **B** explain why many Irish immigrated to Scotland in the 1840s.

Source A

> Irish immigration continued steadily until the 1840s. The Irish potato famine of the mid 1840s however led to a sharp increase in this immigration. It led to great poverty and some landlords evicted those who could not pay their rent. Transport costs were cheap, and wages in the west of Scotland continued to be higher than those in Ireland.

Source B

> In the mid and late 1840s the potato crops in Ireland were destroyed by blight, which caused the death of many people and led many others to leave. Many landlords used the crisis to take away people's homes. The very low wages paid in Ireland meant that the higher wages on offer in Scotland were attractive. Irish people found it was not far to travel to Scotland and that plenty of ships travelled the route, so the cost was cheap. Travelling conditions were miserable.

1. How far do **Sources A** and **B** agree about the reasons for Irish immigration to Scotland? **4**

2. In what ways were Scots encouraged to emigrate between the 1830s and 1930s? **5**

Source C explains why Andrew Carnegie became successful.

> Andrew Carnegie's family left Dunfermline for the USA when Andrew was twelve. He managed to get a job with the Pennsylvania Railroad Company. Here he prospered because of his energy and ability. He began the Company's sleeping car service. He also had great financial skills, borrowing a lot of money to invest. These investments proved to be enormously successful and made it possible for him to buy up iron and steel businesses, coalfields and steamships. In 1901 he sold his businesses to the US Steel Corporation. This made him the richest man in the world.

3. Why did many Scots emigrants, like Andrew Carnegie, became successful abroad? (Use **Source C** and recall.) **5**

[END OF CONTEXT 6]

HISTORICAL STUDY: SCOTTISH AND BRITISH

CONTEXT 7(a): FROM THE CRADLE TO THE GRAVE? SOCIAL WELFARE IN BRITAIN, 1890s–1951

Answer the following questions using recalled knowledge and information from the sources where appropriate.

Sources A and **B** are about the causes of poverty in the early twentieth century.

Source A

> The investigations of Booth and Rowntree both revealed the problems facing the poorer classes in Britain. They identified some of the direct causes of poverty. The main reasons were that a man's earnings were not enough to support himself and his family. They were not able to obtain employment when trade was bad. Some men could not work due to sickness. Bad habits, such as drinking and gambling, also caused problems.

Source B

> Although many people thought Britain was experiencing a golden age, there was increasing unemployment and thirty per cent of the population were living in poverty. Of those living in poverty, about two-thirds were in that position because of low pay or irregular earnings. About one quarter were poor because of illness. Only about one-tenth were poor because of personal failings such as drunkenness or gambling.

1. How far do **Sources A** and **B** agree about the causes of poverty in the early twentieth century? **4**

2. Describe the social reforms of the Liberal government between 1906 and 1914. **5**

Source C is about the Home Front during the Second World War.

> During the Second World War the Home Front was treated and run like a battlefield. The priority was to ensure "fair shares for all" and to avoid waste. The war caused the government to get more involved in all areas of life. The Ministry of Food established the responsibility of the government to ensure the nation's health and safe food supply. War wounded, including bomb victims, were given free treatment. It soon became clear people expected the government to continue to do more for them after the war.

3. Why did the Second World War lead people to expect improvements in social welfare? (Use **Source C** and recall.) **5**

[END OF CONTEXT 7(a)]

HISTORICAL STUDY: SCOTTISH AND BRITISH

CONTEXT 7(b): CAMPAIGNING FOR CHANGE: SOCIAL CHANGE IN SCOTLAND, 1900s–1979

Answer the following questions using recalled knowledge and information from the sources where appropriate.

1. Describe the methods used by women to campaign for the vote in the period 1900 to 1914. **5**

Sources A and **B** are people's memories of going to the cinema in the 1930s.

Source A

> I used to go to the cinema almost every Saturday. We handed over two jam jars which covered the entrance charge of one penny. The action films were quite violent but nobody took them seriously with kids shouting things such as, "Look, the man's got a knife! Mind yer back, Jimmy!" We all enjoyed ourselves enormously and hammered our hands on the plain wooden seats. We must have made an outrageous amount of noise. Looking back, it was basic and in poor condition.

Source B

> For a penny we not only saw the show but sometimes received a free comic or small bag of sweeties as well. The programme comprised of a "funny" and a more dramatic film such as "The Hooded Terror" or "Tarzan", which had plenty of fighting in them. We compared the various cinemas and all agreed that our local was a "flea pit". Some theatres had individual seats instead of benches.

2. How far do **Sources A** and **B** agree about cinema entertainment in the 1930s? **4**

Source C is from a report about Scottish industry after 1945.

Source C

> We have the disadvantage of an outdated railway network and road building is much too slow. Many of the country's factory buildings are greatly in need of modernisation. Many shortages of skilled workers are appearing in industry. We must be ready to accept government and local authority help to solve the problem. To keep up with our competitors abroad, industry must encourage far greater levels of scientific and technical training.

3. Why did Scotland's industries find it difficult to compete with other countries after 1945? (Use **Source C** and recall.) **5**

[END OF CONTEXT 7(b)]

HISTORICAL STUDY: SCOTTISH AND BRITISH

CONTEXT 8: A TIME OF TROUBLES: IRELAND, 1900–1923

Answer the following questions using recalled knowledge and information from the sources where appropriate.

Sources A and **B** are two Irish reactions to the outbreak of the First World War.

Source A

> The interests of Ireland are at stake in this war. Your duty is to fight against Germany and everything it stands for. If we refuse to fight and stay at home then we will be disgracing our nation. Now is not the time for rebellion. By helping Britain, we help ourselves. I call on the men of Ireland to prove their bravery and courage by volunteering for this war.

Source B

> If you are itching to fight, then your duty is to fight for Ireland and not for an empire we do not want to belong to. We have waited long enough. Now is the moment to start the rebellion. We gain nothing by helping the British fight this war. Our interests lie in an independent Ireland and nothing else. Only the foolish and misguided will go to fight in France.

1. How far do **Sources A** and **B** agree about whether or not the Irish should fight in the First World War? **4**

2. Describe the actions taken by both sides in the Anglo-Irish War, 1919–1921. **5**

Source C explains why the 1921 Treaty caused divisions amongst the nationalists.

Source C

> By 1921 most members of the IRA accepted that a war against the British could not be won. Despite this, De Valera encouraged people to reject the Treaty. Moreover, the British were still in Ireland and had not been driven out. His supporters also believed that Ulster should not be partitioned. In particular De Valera objected to the oath of allegiance to the king. Even though the Irish public wanted peace, the anti-treaty forces were prepared to use violence to get what they wanted.

3. Why did some Irish nationalists refuse to accept the 1921 Treaty? (Use **Source C** and recall.) **5**

[END OF CONTEXT 8]

[END OF PART 2: SCOTTISH AND BRITISH CONTEXTS]

Marks

PART 3:

HISTORICAL STUDY: EUROPEAN AND WORLD

CONTEXT 1: THE NORMAN CONQUEST, 1060–1153

Answer the following questions using recalled knowledge and information from the sources where appropriate.

1. What advantages did William have over his enemies at the Battle of Hastings? **5**

Source A explains the influence of Norman England on David I.

Source A

> In 1072 William brought a great army to Scotland in response to Scottish raids on his kingdom. The Scottish king, Malcolm III, agreed to accept William as his overlord. When Malcolm's son David I became king in 1124 he too had to accept this and was determined to copy Norman ways. Furthermore, he had married the Anglo-Norman, Ada de Varene. This brought him estates in Huntingdonshire and Northamptonshire. David saw how the Anglo-Norman king kept a tight grip over England using the nobles to help him govern the country.

2. Why was David I influenced by Norman England? (Use **Source A** and recall.) **5**

Source B is from a charter granting lands to Robert Bruce in 1124.

Source B

> David, by the grace of God, king of the Scots, does hereby give to his faithful servant, Robert Bruce, all the lands of Annandale and the castle of Lochmaben which is to be the centre of the Lordship. In return Robert will provide ten knights fully armed and each with a good horse to fight in the army of the king when called upon to do so.

3. How useful is **Source B** as evidence of the importance of the Bruce lords of Annandale? **4**

[END OF CONTEXT 1]

HISTORICAL STUDY: EUROPEAN AND WORLD

CONTEXT 2: THE CROSS AND THE CRESCENT: THE FIRST CRUSADE, 1096–1125

Answer the following questions using recalled knowledge and information from the sources where appropriate.

Source A was written by Abbot Guibert, who interviewed followers of Peter the Hermit.

Source A

> I do not remember any other man being held in such honour. Peter was generous to the poor and brought peace to every village he visited. He had great authority and a wonderful ability as a speaker. He seemed so holy that even the hairs from his donkey's tail were plucked as relics.

1. How useful is **Source A** as evidence of the popularity of Peter the Hermit? **4**

2. What problems did the Crusaders face on their journey from Europe to Jerusalem? **5**

Source B explains why Jerusalem was difficult to capture.

Source B

> Massive walls and flanking towers surrounded the city of Jerusalem. Starving the garrison into surrender was not easy because those inside had prepared well for an attack. They used drainage systems to reduce the possibility of disease. They had large water cisterns to provide them with a good supply of water. Although the Crusaders were overjoyed at seeing the Holy City, they knew they had an enormous task to complete.

3. Why did the First Crusade find Jerusalem difficult to capture? (Use **Source B** and recall.) **5**

[END OF CONTEXT 2]

HISTORICAL STUDY: EUROPEAN AND WORLD

CONTEXT 3: WAR, DEATH AND REVOLT IN MEDIEVAL EUROPE, 1328–1436

Answer the following questions using recalled knowledge and information from the sources where appropriate.

1. Describe the campaigns of the Black Prince in France. 5

Source A is about the reasons for discontent among the French peasants in 1358.

Source A

> France suffered a humiliating defeat in 1358. The English leaders withdrew to Bordeaux and agreed to a truce. During this time the great companies of mercenaries from the English forces pillaged the French countryside. The French peasants were further enraged by the nobles' demands for heavier payments of feudal dues and by the order of the Dauphin Charles that the peasants rebuild the castles of their aristocratic oppressors.

2. Why did the French peasants revolt in 1358? (Use **Source A** and recall.) 5

Source B is from an account of the Peasants' Revolt in England in the Anonimalle Chronicle written in the late fourteenth century.

Source B

> At this time the common people had as their advisor an evil churchman named John Ball. He advised them to get rid of all the lords, archbishops, abbots and priors. He said that the wealth of these men should be distributed among the people. He was respected by the commoners as a prophet and he worked to increase their hatred.

3. How useful is **Source B** as evidence of the aims of the Peasants' Revolt of 1381? 4

[END OF CONTEXT 3]

HISTORICAL STUDY: EUROPEAN AND WORLD

CONTEXT 4: NEW WORLDS: EUROPE IN THE AGE OF EXPANSION, 1480s–1530s

Answer the following questions using recalled knowledge and information from the sources where appropriate.

Source A explains why the Europeans wanted to expand overseas.

Source A

> Each of the European states began exploration at different times. To increase their wealth they began to explore in search of a variety of products to trade. In the North Atlantic Ocean, an enormously valuable trade in fish encouraged boats of all European nations to search for fishing grounds farther from Europe. Spices drew explorers around the tip of Africa to Southeast Asia because they needed spices to preserve the meat they ate. By trading directly with the East, Europeans could avoid costly customs duties, or taxes, charged by rulers of every country.

1. Why did European countries want to explore overseas between 1480 and 1540? (Use **Source A** and recall.)   5

Source B is from a letter from the African ruler, King Affonso of Angola, to the king of Portugal in the sixteenth century.

Source B

> We cannot say how great the damage is since Portuguese merchants seize our people, sons of farmers, sons of nobles, servants and relatives daily. They also wish to take the goods and produce of this kingdom. They grab them and sell them. Their wickedness and evil is so great that our country is losing its entire people.

2. How useful is **Source B** as evidence of the effects of Portugal's exploration of Africa?   4

3. Describe the methods used by the Spanish Conquistadors to defeat either the **Aztecs** or the **Incas**.   5

[END OF CONTEXT 4]

Marks

HISTORICAL STUDY: EUROPEAN AND WORLD

CONTEXT 5: "TEA AND FREEDOM": THE AMERICAN REVOLUTION, 1763–1783

Answer the following questions using recalled knowledge and information from the sources where appropriate.

1. Describe the complaints of the American colonists against British rule. **5**

Source A is an extract from the diary of one of George Washington's army surgeons, in 1777.

Source A

> The army now begins to grow sickly from the continued tiredness they have suffered during this campaign. Poor food, hard living conditions, cold weather, nasty clothes, nasty food and vomiting out of my senses, I tell you the devil's in it. I can't endure it. Why are we sent here to starve and freeze?

2. How useful is **Source A** as evidence of the poor condition of Washington's Continental Army at the start of the War of Independence? **4**

Source B explains why Britain lost the American war.

Source B

> When the revolution began, Britain was a great power with an experienced army and a strong navy. It had economic resources and a king determined to keep the colonies intact. However things went wrong. Britain never had a clear strategy for winning the war. Supply and communication were also problems. In addition to this, Washington was able to hold his army together and maintained morale. At home the British Parliament was not united behind the war.

3. Why did the British lose the war with the American colonists? (Use **Source B** and recall.) **5**

[END OF CONTEXT 5]

HISTORICAL STUDY: EUROPEAN AND WORLD

CONTEXT 6: "THIS ACCURSED TRADE": THE BRITISH SLAVE TRADE AND ITS ABOLITION, 1770–1807

Answer the following questions using recalled knowledge and information from the sources where appropriate.

Source A is from a book by Mungo Park, an eighteenth century explorer in Africa.

Source A

> The African captives are usually secured by putting the right leg of one and the left leg of another into the same pair of fetters. By supporting the fetters with a string, they can just walk, though very slowly. Every four slaves are likewise fastened together by their necks with a strong rope or twisted thongs and at night extra fetters are put on their hands.

1. How useful is **Source A** as evidence of the treatment of Africans when they were first captured? **4**

2. Describe what happened to slaves at the end of the Middle Passage. **5**

Source B is about the campaign to abolish the slave trade.

Source B

> In 1787 a small group of Quakers launched a public campaign against the British slave trade. Baptists and Methodists found a new social and political voice by supporting the campaign. Slavery seemed offensive in the world after the French Revolution, when more and more people talked of liberty. British manufacturers now supported the idea of free labour. At last many people saw the approach of the end of such an abominable practice.

3. Why was the slave trade abolished in 1807? (Use **Source B** and recall.) **5**

[END OF CONTEXT 6]

HISTORICAL STUDY: EUROPEAN AND WORLD

CONTEXT 7: CITIZENS! THE FRENCH REVOLUTION, 1789–1794

Answer the following questions using recalled knowledge and information from the sources where appropriate.

Source A is about the ideas of the "Philosophers" who questioned the way France was ruled in 1789.

Source A

> Diderot declared that governments should be influenced by scientific ideas and not just the will of the king. Montesquieu stated that power should be shared between the monarchy and parliament. He argued that the making of laws and raising taxes should be the role of parliament. Many Frenchmen learned of Montesquieu's ideas when they were sent to help in the American War of Independence. Rousseau attacked the idea that the king and the nobles were born to rule over the people.

1. Why did new ideas encourage people to question the way France was ruled in 1789? (Use **Source A** and recall.) **5**

2. Describe the events leading up to the storming of the Bastille in July 1789. **5**

Source B is a description of the execution of Louis XVI by one of the men who sentenced him to death, written in 1792.

Source B

> His blood flows and there is a cry of joy as 80,000 armed men cheer. His blood flows and there are people who dip a fingertip or scrap of paper in it. An executioner sells small bundles of his hair and people buy ribbons to tie it with. Everyone carries off a small bloodstained fragment of his clothing.

3. How useful is **Source B** as evidence of how people felt about Louis XVI's death? **4**

[END OF CONTEXT 7]

HISTORICAL STUDY: EUROPEAN AND WORLD

CONTEXT 8: CAVOUR, GARIBALDI AND THE MAKING OF ITALY, 1815–1870

Answer the following questions using recalled knowledge and information from the sources where appropriate.

Source A is from a poem by the Italian nationalist Leopardi. It was written in 1818.

Source A

> O my fatherland, I see the greatness that was Rome
> And the arches and the columns and
> The marble towers of our Roman ancestors
> Where is that glory now?

1. How useful is **Source A** as evidence of the growth of nationalist feeling in Italy after 1815?

2. Describe the difficulties faced by the Italian nationalists during the revolutions of 1848–1849.

Source B explains the development of Piedmont in the 1850s.

Source B

> In 1851 Piedmont signed trade agreements with France, Britain and Belgium. This resulted in a growth in trade. Between 1850 and 1859 imports and exports grew by 300%. By this time 850 kilometres of railway track were in operation in Piedmont. In 1853 an electric telegraph link was set up between Turin and Paris. A canal building programme began in 1857 which helped the growth of industry. By 1859 Piedmont was considered to be the most modern state in Italy.

3. Why had Piedmont become a wealthy and powerful state by 1859? (Use **Source B** and recall.)

[END OF CONTEXT 8]

HISTORICAL STUDY: EUROPEAN AND WORLD

CONTEXT 9: IRON AND BLOOD? BISMARCK AND THE CREATION OF THE GERMAN EMPIRE, 1815–1871

Answer the following questions using recalled knowledge and information from the sources where appropriate.

1. Describe the growth of nationalism in the German states between 1815 and 1850. **5**

Source A is about the failure of the 1848 revolutions.

Source A

> In 1848 revolutions broke out all over Europe. In Germany there were wide differences in the aims of the revolutionaries. The liberals wanted a united German Empire with a national parliament. Other groups didn't want to abolish the monarchy but wanted to give more power to the ordinary people. They could not agree about the borders of the new Germany. It is therefore no surprise that the 1848 revolutions collapsed.

2. Why did the 1848 revolutions in Germany fail? (Use **Source A** and recall.) **5**

Source B is from a letter written by Bismarck to the King of Prussia in 1866.

Source B

> We have to avoid punishing Austria too severely because we do not want her to be bitter and wanting revenge. We ought to keep the possibility of becoming friends again. If Austria is punished she will become the ally of France and every other country who is opposed to us.

3. How useful is **Source B** as evidence of why Prussia wanted a lenient treaty after the Austro-Prussian War in 1866? **4**

[END OF CONTEXT 9]

HISTORICAL STUDY: EUROPEAN AND WORLD

CONTEXT 10: THE RED FLAG: LENIN AND THE RUSSIAN REVOLUTION, 1894–1921

Answer the following questions using recalled knowledge and information from the sources where appropriate.

Source A is about Stolypin's agricultural reforms.

Source A

> Peasants were allowed to buy up strips of land from their neighbours to make a single land holding. Stolypin set up a peasants' bank to provide loans for them to do this. This would also allow them to use more modern methods of agriculture. Stolypin believed that this would create a new class of prosperous "kulaks" who would be loyal to the government. About 15% of peasants took up the offer and made greater profits when grain production increased.

1. Why did the lives of some peasants improve as a result of Stolypin's reforms? (Use **Source A** and recall.) **5**

2. Describe the problems facing the Provisional Government in 1917. **5**

Source B is from the diary of a French diplomat living in Russia in February 1918.

Source B

> We are now living in a madhouse. In the last few days there has been an avalanche of decrees. First comes a decree cancelling all banking transactions, then comes one confiscating housing. A law is made to take the children of middle class parents into care. In this way differences in education will be avoided.

3. How useful is **Source B** as evidence of life in Russia after the Bolshevik revolution? **4**

[END OF CONTEXT 10]

HISTORICAL STUDY: EUROPEAN AND WORLD

CONTEXT 11: FREE AT LAST? RACE RELATIONS IN THE USA, 1918–1968

Answer the following questions using recalled knowledge and information from the sources where appropriate.

1. Describe the effects of the Jim Crow laws on Black Americans. **5**

Source A is about the events in Birmingham, Alabama, in 1963.

Source A

> In January 1963, Martin Luther King announced that the SCLC was going to Birmingham, Alabama, the most racist city in America. King knew that civil rights protesters would be risking their lives when they arrived in Birmingham. Racists had the support of the Birmingham police department. King knew if they could lead a successful demonstration in Birmingham they might spark off big changes across the South. On May 2 the march began and the police were waiting for them. Over nine hundred children were jailed that day.

2. Why was the protest in Birmingham in 1963 an important event in the civil rights campaign in the USA? (Use **Source A** and recall.) **5**

Source B is from a speech by Stokely Carmichael in Greenwood on 17 June 1966.

Source B

> This is the twenty-seventh time I have been arrested – and I ain't going to jail no more. The only way we gonna stop them white men from whuppin' us is to take over. We been saying freedom for six years and we ain't got nothin'. What we gonna start saying now is Black Power.

3. How useful is **Source B** as evidence of the beliefs of the Black Power movement? **4**

[END OF CONTEXT 11]

HISTORICAL STUDY: EUROPEAN AND WORLD

CONTEXT 12: THE ROAD TO WAR, 1933–1939

Answer the following questions using recalled knowledge and information from the sources where appropriate.

1. In what ways did Hitler increase German military power in the years after 1933?

Source A is the opinion of Lord Tweedsmuir, a British politician, about the Anschluss, March 1938.

Source A

> I don't see what the problem is. Austria will be much happier as part of Germany. The Treaty of Versailles said that Germany and Austria must never unite but that was foolish. Some people say that Czechoslovakia will be Hitler's next target but that is not our problem.

2. How useful is **Source A** as evidence of British attitudes to the Anschluss?

Source B explains German complaints against Poland.

Source B

> Germany had signed a non-aggression treaty with Poland in 1934 which made Poland feel safe. Yet this was the country that the Nazis hated most of all and not just for racial reasons. The creation of Poland meant that large areas of land had been taken from Germany and because of this millions of Germans were forced to live under Polish rule. The German city of Danzig had been taken away from Germany and was run by the League of Nations to suit the Poles.

3. Why did Germany declare war on Poland in 1939? (Use **Source B** and recall.)

[END OF CONTEXT 12]

HISTORICAL STUDY: EUROPEAN AND WORLD

CONTEXT 13: IN THE SHADOW OF THE BOMB: THE COLD WAR, 1945–1985

Answer the following questions using recalled knowledge and information from the sources where appropriate.

Source A is from a document by President Kennedy on the situation in Berlin in 1961.

Source A

> It seems particularly stupid to risk killing a million Americans over an argument about access rights on a motorway or because the Germans want Germany reunited. If I'm going to threaten Russia with nuclear war, it will have to be for much bigger and more important reasons than that.

1. How useful is **Source A** as evidence of American policy towards the Berlin Crisis in 1961? — 4

2. Describe the part played by the USA in the Cuban Missile Crisis of 1962. — 5

Source B explains why the USA lost the war in Vietnam.

Source B

> North Vietnam suffered widespread destruction but it still triumphed. America realised too late that the real war in Vietnam was not just a military one but one for "the hearts and minds" of the peasants. American troops failed to cope with the guerrilla tactics of the Viet Cong. The communists were backed militarily by China and Russia. By the late 1960s all that the American troops wanted was to go home.

3. Why did the USA lose the war in Vietnam? (Use **Source B** and recall.) — 5

[END OF CONTEXT 13]
[END OF PART 3: EUROPEAN AND WORLD CONTEXTS]
[END OF QUESTION PAPER]

INTERMEDIATE 2
2009

[BLANK PAGE]

X044/201

NATIONAL QUALIFICATIONS 2009

TUESDAY, 2 JUNE 9.00 AM – 10.45 AM

HISTORY INTERMEDIATE 2

The instructions for this paper are on *Page two*. Read them carefully before you begin your answers.
Some sources in this examination have been adapted or translated.

INSTRUCTIONS

Answer **one** question from Part 1, The Short Essay

Answer **one** context* from Part 2, Scottish and British

Answer **one** context* from Part 3, European and World

Answer **one** other context* from

- **either** Part 2, Scottish and British

- **or** Part 3, European and World

*Answer all the questions in each of your chosen contexts.

Contents

Part 1 Short Essay Questions.
Answer **one** question only. Pages 4–6

Part 2 Scottish and British Contexts

1. Murder in the Cathedral: Crown, Church and People, 1154–1173 — Page 8
2. Wallace, Bruce and the Wars of Independence, 1286–1328 — Page 9
3. Mary, Queen of Scots and the Scottish Reformation, 1540s–1587 — Page 10
4. The Coming of the Civil War, 1603–1642 — Page 11
5. "Ane End of Ane Auld Sang": Scotland and the Treaty of Union, 1690s–1715 — Page 12
6. Immigrants and Exiles: Scotland, 1830s–1930s — Page 13
7.(a) From the Cradle to the Grave? Social Welfare in Britain, 1890s–1951 — Page 14

OR

7.(b) Campaigning for Change: Social Change in Scotland, 1900s–1979 — Page 15
8. A Time of Troubles: Ireland, 1900–1923 — Page 16

Part 3 European and World Contexts

1. The Norman Conquest, 1060–1153 — Page 17
2. The Cross and the Crescent: The First Crusade, 1096–1125 — Page 18
3. War, Death and Revolt in Medieval Europe, 1328–1436 — Page 19
4. New Worlds: Europe in the Age of Expansion, 1480s–1530s — Page 20
5. "Tea and Freedom": The American Revolution, 1763–1783 — Page 21
6. "This Accursed Trade": The British Slave Trade and its Abolition, 1770–1807 — Page 22
7. Citizens! The French Revolution, 1789–1794 — Page 23
8. Cavour, Garibaldi and the Making of Italy, 1815–1870 — Page 24
9. Iron and Blood? Bismarck and the Creation of the German Empire, 1815–1871 — Page 25
10. The Red Flag: Lenin and the Russian Revolution, 1894–1921 — Page 26
11. Free at Last? Race Relations in the USA, 1918–1968 — Page 27
12. The Road to War, 1933–1939 — Page 28
13. In the Shadow of the Bomb: The Cold War, 1945–1985 — Page 29

[Turn over

PART 1: THE SHORT ESSAY

Answer **one** question. For this question you should write a short essay using your own knowledge. The essay should include an introduction, development and conclusion. Each question is worth 8 marks.

SCOTTISH AND BRITISH CONTEXTS:

CONTEXT 1: MURDER IN THE CATHEDRAL: CROWN, CHURCH AND PEOPLE, 1154–1173

Question 1: Explain why knights were important in the twelfth century. — 8

CONTEXT 2: WALLACE, BRUCE AND THE WARS OF INDEPENDENCE, 1286–1328

Question 2: Explain why John Balliol lost his position as King of Scots in 1296. — 8

CONTEXT 3: MARY, QUEEN OF SCOTS AND THE SCOTTISH REFORMATION, 1540s–1587

Question 3: Explain why Mary, Queen of Scots, faced difficulties ruling Scotland when she returned in 1561. — 8

CONTEXT 4: THE COMING OF THE CIVIL WAR, 1603–1642

Question 4: Explain why there were problems between Crown and Parliament during the reign of James VI and I. — 8

CONTEXT 5: "ANE END OF ANE AULD SANG": SCOTLAND AND THE TREATY OF UNION, 1690s–1715

Question 5: Explain why there was so much opposition to a Union in Scotland before 1707. — 8

CONTEXT 6: IMMIGRANTS AND EXILES: SCOTLAND, 1830s–1930s

Question 6: Explain why Scots emigrants made a valuable contribution in Canada and the United States. — 8

CONTEXT 7(a): FROM THE CRADLE TO THE GRAVE? SOCIAL WELFARE IN BRITAIN, 1890s–1951

Question 7(a): Explain why the Liberal reforms, 1906–1914, failed to solve the problems of the poor. — 8

	Marks
CONTEXT 7(b): CAMPAIGNING FOR CHANGE: SOCIAL CHANGE IN SCOTLAND, 1900s–1979	
Question 7(b): Explain why many industries in Scotland experienced problems in the years between the two world wars.	8

CONTEXT 8: A TIME OF TROUBLES: IRELAND, 1900–1923	
Question 8: Explain why support for Sinn Fein increased after 1916.	8

EUROPEAN AND WORLD CONTEXTS:

CONTEXT 1: THE NORMAN CONQUEST, 1060–1153	
Question 9: Explain why David I introduced feudalism to Scotland.	8

CONTEXT 2: THE CROSS AND THE CRESCENT: THE FIRST CRUSADE, 1096–1125	
Question 10: Explain why Pope Urban II called the First Crusade.	8

CONTEXT 3: WAR, DEATH AND REVOLT IN MEDIEVAL EUROPE, 1328–1436	
Question 11: Explain why the Hundred Years' War broke out between England and France in 1337.	8

CONTEXT 4: NEW WORLDS: EUROPE IN THE AGE OF EXPANSION, 1480s–1530s	
Question 12: Explain why European countries wanted to search for new lands between the 1480s and 1530s.	8

CONTEXT 5: "TEA AND FREEDOM": THE AMERICAN REVOLUTION, 1763–1783	
Question 13: Explain why the colonists won the American War of Independence.	8

CONTEXT 6: "THIS ACCURSED TRADE": THE BRITISH SLAVE TRADE AND ITS ABOLITION, 1770–1807	
Question 14: Explain why there was increasing support for the campaign against the slave trade by the 1780s.	8

[Turn over

CONTEXT 7: CITIZENS! THE FRENCH REVOLUTION, 1789–1794

Question 15: Explain why few French people supported Louis XVI in 1789.

8

CONTEXT 8: CAVOUR, GARIBALDI AND THE MAKING OF ITALY, 1815–1870

Question 16: Explain why Cavour was important to Italian unification.

8

CONTEXT 9: IRON AND BLOOD? BISMARCK AND THE CREATION OF THE GERMAN EMPIRE, 1815–1871

Question 17: Explain why Bismarck's leadership was important to the unification of the German states.

8

CONTEXT 10: THE RED FLAG: LENIN AND THE RUSSIAN REVOLUTION, 1894–1921

Question 18: Explain why the Reds won the Civil War.

8

CONTEXT 11: FREE AT LAST? RACE RELATIONS IN THE USA, 1918–1968

Question 19: Explain why black people rioted in many American cities in the 1960s.

8

CONTEXT 12: THE ROAD TO WAR, 1933–1939

Question 20: Explain why events after Munich, September 1938, led to the outbreak of war in 1939.

8

CONTEXT 13: IN THE SHADOW OF THE BOMB: THE COLD WAR, 1945–1985

Question 21: Explain why the USA became involved in a crisis over Cuba in 1962.

8

[END OF PART 1: THE SHORT ESSAY]

[Turn over for PART 2: SCOTTISH AND BRITISH CONTEXTS on *Page eight*

PART 2:

HISTORICAL STUDY: SCOTTISH AND BRITISH

CONTEXT 1: MURDER IN THE CATHEDRAL: CROWN, CHURCH AND PEOPLE, 1154–1173

Answer the following questions using recalled knowledge and information from the sources where appropriate.

Source A was written in 1177 by Peter of Blois, Henry II's secretary.

Source A

> Every day the king travels around his kingdom. He never rests and works tirelessly to make sure that his people are at peace. On occasion, he attacks the barons but this is only so that the law of the country can be upheld. No one is more honest, more polite and more generous to the poor than the king. He is truly loved by his people.

1. How useful is **Source A** as evidence of the character of Henry II? — 4

2. Describe the life of a monk in medieval times. — 5

Source B explains why Henry II and Archbishop Becket quarrelled.

Source B

> Henry II appointed Thomas Becket as Archbishop of Canterbury in 1162. Almost immediately their friendship was tested when Becket resigned as Chancellor. Until then Becket had been a loyal servant, so this action stunned the king. Becket then refused to sign the Constitutions of Clarendon and would not agree to reduce the power of the Church. When summoned to appear at the Northampton trial, Becket fled to France without the king's permission. He remained there for six years protected by the king of France.

3. Why did Henry II and Archbishop Becket quarrel? (Use **Source B** and recall.) — 5

[END OF CONTEXT 1]

HISTORICAL STUDY: SCOTTISH AND BRITISH

CONTEXT 2: WALLACE, BRUCE AND THE WARS OF INDEPENDENCE, 1286–1328

Answer the following questions using recalled knowledge and information from the sources where appropriate.

Source A was written by a Scottish chronicler some time after the death of Alexander III in 1286.

Source A

> On 19th March, the king was delayed by the ferry at South Queensferry until dusk on a dark, stormy night. When advised by his companions not to go beyond Inverkeithing that night, he rejected their advice and with an escort of knights he hurried along a very steep track towards Kinghorn. To the west of that place, his horse stumbled and he was killed.

1. How useful is **Source A** as evidence about the death of King Alexander III? 4

2. Describe what happened at the Battle of Stirling Bridge. 5

Source B explains why the Scots sent the Declaration of Arbroath to the Pope in 1320.

Source B

> In the years after Bannockburn, although Bruce controlled Scotland, he was not accepted internationally as its king. Earlier efforts to gain recognition by invading the north of England had failed. They had only annoyed Edward. The Scots then tried to increase the pressure on Edward by invading Ireland, but this ended in disaster when Edward Bruce was killed in 1318. When they sent the declaration to the Pope in 1320, they hoped he would recognise Bruce as king.

3. Why did the Scots send the Declaration of Arbroath to the Pope in 1320? (Use **Source B** and recall.) 5

[END OF CONTEXT 2]

HISTORICAL STUDY: SCOTTISH AND BRITISH

CONTEXT 3: MARY, QUEEN OF SCOTS AND THE SCOTTISH REFORMATION, 1540s–1587

Answer the following questions using recalled knowledge and information from the sources where appropriate.

Source A explains why Protestantism spread in Scotland in the 1540s and 1550s.

Source A

> In Germany, the ideas of Martin Luther had started the Reformation movement. Some Scots began questioning the teachings of the Catholic Church. During the Rough Wooing, English invaders had encouraged this by distributing English translations of the Bible so people could study the Bible for themselves. The Catholic Church continued to use the Latin Bible. Religious pamphlets, smuggled into Scotland from Europe, also spread Protestant ideas. The "Good and Godly Ballads" made these ideas popular. Protestantism began to spread more quickly in Scotland.

1. Why did Protestantism spread in Scotland in the 1540s and 1550s? (Use **Source A** and recall.) **5**

2. Describe the events surrounding the murder of Darnley in 1567. **5**

Source B is part of a letter written by Mary, Queen of Scots, to Queen Elizabeth in 1582.

Source B

> While I was in Scotland, my subjects were encouraged to speak, act and finally to rebel against me by the agents, spies and secret messengers sent there in your name. I do not have any specific proof of that except for the confession of one person whom you rewarded very generously for his hard work at that time.

3. How useful is **Source B** as evidence of Mary's opinion of Queen Elizabeth? **4**

[END OF CONTEXT 3]

HISTORICAL STUDY: SCOTTISH AND BRITISH

CONTEXT 4: THE COMING OF THE CIVIL WAR, 1603–1642

Answer the following questions using recalled knowledge and information from the sources where appropriate.

Source A is from "A Concise History of Scotland" by Fitzroy McLean, published in 1974.

Source A

> The new service book was read for the first time in St Giles on 23 July 1637 amid scenes of violence which soon developed into a riot. Tradition says the females of the congregation played a leading part, egged on by a certain Jenny Geddes. Before long, the Privy Council were forced to shut themselves in Holyroodhouse to escape the mob.

1. How useful is **Source A** as evidence of how the Scots reacted to Charles I's introduction of the Common Prayer Book in 1637? **4**

Source B explains why Charles I became unpopular in England between 1629 and 1640.

Source B

> Since the Middle Ages, only people who lived near the coast had to pay Ship Money. In 1635 Charles I made people from inland areas pay Ship Money tax as well. There were strong objections because the king had imposed this new tax without the consent of Parliament. He also fined people who had built on common land, or in royal forests. Anyone who refused to pay was tried in special courts. The king was seen as a tyrant. People turned against him.

2. Explain why Charles I became unpopular in England between 1629 and 1640. (Use **Source B** and recall.) **5**

3. Describe the events between 1640 and 1642 which led to the outbreak of the Civil War. **5**

[END OF CONTEXT 4]

HISTORICAL STUDY: SCOTTISH AND BRITISH

CONTEXT 5: "ANE END OF ANE AULD SANG": SCOTLAND AND THE TREATY OF UNION, 1690s–1715

Answer the following questions using recalled knowledge and information from the sources where appropriate.

Source A is a public notice published by the Directors of the Company of Scotland in 1698.

Source A

> The Court of Directors now have ships ready and loaded with provisions and all manner of things needed for their intended expedition to settle a colony in the Indies. They give notice that to encourage people to go on this expedition, they promise to give them fifty acres of good ground to grow their crops.

1. How useful is **Source A** as evidence about Scottish preparations for the Darien Expedition? **4**

Source B explains why many Scottish nobles agreed to the Act of Union.

Source B

> The Scottish nobility has been criticised for "betraying" Scotland at the time of the Union. There was, however, a considerable effort put into convincing them of the wealth which a Union would bring to Scotland. They would prosper by having access to England's colonies and after the Union many did invest in the sugar trade of the West Indies. Besides, a Union would guarantee the Protestant Succession and its supporters would gain both royal approval and the benefits it brought.

2. Why did many Scottish nobles agree to the Act of Union? (Use **Source B** and recall.) **5**

3. In what ways did Scotland change as a result of the Act of Union? **5**

[END OF CONTEXT 5]

HISTORICAL STUDY: SCOTTISH AND BRITISH

CONTEXT 6: IMMIGRANTS AND EXILES: SCOTLAND, 1830s–1930s

Answer the following questions using recalled knowledge and information from the sources where appropriate.

Source A is evidence given to a government enquiry in 1836 by a Catholic priest in Aberdeen.

Source A

> The number of cotton and linen factories in Aberdeen has continued to grow since the Irish people were encouraged to come to us. Finding work is easy and fairly good wages are offered to them in these factories. A considerable number of Irish people have come to the city and have brought their families with them.

1. How useful is **Source A** as evidence of the reasons Irish people came to Scotland after 1830? **4**

2. Describe the experience of Irish immigrants in the west of Scotland. **5**

Source B explains why many Scots emigrated overseas in the twentieth century.

Source B

> Mr Macdonald, the headmaster, said that he had faith in Canada. Many of his best pupils who were now living in Canada were succeeding. This was obvious from the money and letters they sent home to their parents. He then introduced the Canadian immigration agent, who spoke first in Gaelic and then in English. He said Canada was a huge country which offered great opportunities for farming. He enthusiastically praised the country as he showed view after view of scenes of Canada on the screen.

3. Why did many Scots emigrate overseas in the twentieth century? (Use **Source B** and recall.) **5**

[END OF CONTEXT 6]

HISTORICAL STUDY: SCOTTISH AND BRITISH

CONTEXT 7(a): FROM THE CRADLE TO THE GRAVE? SOCIAL WELFARE IN BRITAIN, 1890s–1951

Answer the following questions using recalled knowledge and information from the sources where appropriate.

Source A comments on changing attitudes towards poverty.

Source A

> By the start of the twentieth century, attitudes towards the poor in Britain were changing. Trade unions felt the Liberals and Conservatives did not do enough for the poor. There was also a growth in Socialist thinking which felt very strongly that a high level of poverty was wrong. The Labour Party was formed in 1900. It stood for practical reforms to tackle poverty. The Labour Party threatened to take support away from the Liberals. Frightened by this, the Liberals began to think of ways to help the poor.

1. Why did attitudes towards poverty change in the early twentieth century? (Use **Source A** and recall.) **5**

Source B is a cartoon from the Daily Herald newspaper in 1942.

Source B

2. How useful is **Source B** as evidence of the ideas in the Beveridge Report? **4**

3. Describe the reforms introduced by Labour after 1945 to improve the lives of the British people. **5**

[END OF CONTEXT 7(a)]

HISTORICAL STUDY: SCOTTISH AND BRITISH

CONTEXT 7(b): CAMPAIGNING FOR CHANGE: SOCIAL CHANGE IN SCOTLAND, 1900s–1979

Marks

Answer the following questions using recalled knowledge and information from the sources where appropriate.

1. Describe the ways sport became more popular in Scotland between 1900 and 1939. **5**

Source A explains why women had not gained the right to vote by 1914.

Source A

> In the years before the Great War, the government had a number of problems to deal with and did not regard votes for women as very important. In addition, the Prime Minister, Mr Asquith, was personally opposed to giving women the franchise. Emmeline Pankhurst founded the Women's Social and Political Union even though most men believed that women should not get involved in politics. When women began militant actions such as breaking shop windows, they were accused of being irresponsible.

2. Why had women not gained the right to vote by 1914? (Use **Source A** and recall.) **5**

Source B is a photograph of a class being taught to wash clothes in a Dundee school in 1938.

Source B

3. How useful is **Source B** as evidence of the way Scottish children were educated in the 1930s? **4**

[END OF CONTEXT 7(b)]

HISTORICAL STUDY: SCOTTISH AND BRITISH

CONTEXT 8: A TIME OF TROUBLES: IRELAND, 1900–1923

Answer the following questions using recalled knowledge and information from the sources where appropriate.

Source A explains why the Ulster Unionists were against Home Rule for Ireland.

Source A

> Unionists knew that the Home Rule Bill could not be defeated in parliament. The Unionists argued that Home Rule would destroy their way of life. Ulster was far richer than the rest of Ireland and many believed that they would be forced into poverty if the law was accepted. Led by MPs such as Edward Carson, as many as 50,000 Unionists attended meetings in Belfast. They were afraid that Ulster would be isolated from the Empire and that the Protestant Church could be weakened.

1. Why were the Ulster Unionists against Home Rule for Ireland? (Use **Source A** and recall.) **5**

Source B is a poster produced by the Irish National Party in 1915.

Source B

2. How useful is **Source B** as evidence of Irish Nationalists' attitudes towards the First World War? **4**

3. Describe the Civil War which broke out in Ireland in 1922. **5**

[END OF CONTEXT 8]

[END OF PART 2: SCOTTISH AND BRITISH CONTEXTS]

PART 3:

HISTORICAL STUDY: EUROPEAN AND WORLD

CONTEXT 1: THE NORMAN CONQUEST, 1060–1153

Answer the following questions using recalled knowledge and information from the sources where appropriate.

Sources A and **B** are about Earl Harold's right to become King of England in 1066.

Source A

> King Edward died in London having reigned for twenty three years. The next day he was buried amid the bitter grieving of all present. After the burial, Harold, whom Edward had nominated as his rightful successor, was chosen as King by all the powerful lords of England and on the same day was crowned legitimately and with great ceremony by Aldred, Archbishop of York.

Source B

> Harold did not wait for public support but broke the oath he had taken to support William's rightful claim to the throne. With the help of a few of his supporters, he seized the throne on the day of Edward's funeral at the very time when all the people were mourning their loss. He was illegally crowned by Stigund of Canterbury, who had been excommunicated by the Pope.

1. How far do **Sources A** and **B** disagree about Harold's right to be King of England? **4**

2. Describe the methods used by William to increase his royal authority. **5**

Source C explains why there was an increase in the number of abbeys and monasteries in Scotland.

Source C

> David was the youngest son of the saintly Queen Margaret and was very religious. He began a building of abbeys and monasteries such as would never be known again in Scotland. Much of the wealth that David gained from his burghs was poured into these great new projects. David encouraged his nobles to leave land to the church. Master craftsmen were brought from England and France. The kingdom was alive with a new spirit and his work was carried on by the kings that followed.

3. Why did the number of abbeys and monasteries in Scotland increase during the reign of David I? (Use **Source C** and recall.) **5**

[END OF CONTEXT 1]

HISTORICAL STUDY: EUROPEAN AND WORLD

CONTEXT 2: THE CROSS AND THE CRESCENT: THE FIRST CRUSADE, 1096–1125

Answer the following questions using recalled knowledge and information from the sources where appropriate.

Source **A** explains why the Peoples' Crusade failed.

Source A

> After months of travelling, Peter the Hermit arrived at Constantinople. The journey had been difficult and many in his army had already been killed. Emperor Alexius warned the Crusaders not to attack the Muslims but to wait for the knights. The Crusaders were eager to get to Jerusalem and so ignored this advice. Soon afterwards, the Crusaders began arguing amongst themselves. They elected their own leaders and no longer listened to Peter the Hermit. In despair he left the Crusade and returned to Constantinople.

1. Why did the Peoples' Crusade fail? (Use **Source A** and recall.) — 5

2. Describe the capture of Nicaea by the First Crusade. — 5

Sources **B** and **C** describe the Crusaders' victory at Antioch.

Source B

> Kerbogha and the Muslim forces attacked the Crusaders the minute they left the city. Bohemond led the Crusaders and organised the knights. Without his leadership they would have been defeated. Although they were tired and hungry, they continued to fight. The Muslims were brave and did not give up. Eventually the Crusaders forced them to flee the battlefield and won a great victory.

Source C

> Although the Muslim forces surrounded Antioch, they did not attack the Crusaders when they left the city. Bohemond commanded the army but could not organise his knights and was nearly defeated. The Crusaders were only victorious because the Muslims did not respect Kerbogha. They refused to fight and fled the battlefield. Their cowardly behaviour meant the Muslims lost the battle.

3. How far do **Sources B** and **C** disagree about the Crusaders' victory at Antioch? — 4

[END OF CONTEXT 2]

HISTORICAL STUDY: EUROPEAN AND WORLD

CONTEXT 3: WAR, DEATH AND REVOLT IN MEDIEVAL EUROPE, 1328–1436

Answer the following questions using recalled knowledge and information from the sources where appropriate.

Source A explains why the Black Death spread across Europe in the fourteenth century.

Source A

> When a rat died of plague its fleas would leave and carry the disease to humans. This happened because humans and rats lived close together. Trading ships were often infested with rats. If these rats died of plague their fleas could give it to sailors and the people in the ports. A ship would therefore carry the plague until the sailors died of it. Diseased rats could also get into merchants' wagons and be carried across the country. This explanation of the spread of the plague is called the trade route theory.

1. Why did the Black Death spread across Europe in the fourteenth century? (Use **Source A** and recall.)   **5**

Sources B and **C** describe the role of Henry V in the Hundred Years' War.

Source B

> Henry V was the last great Plantagenet king. He believed strongly in his right to the French throne and convinced many Frenchmen that his cause was just. His great speech to his archers before Agincourt inspired victory. He was a leader who expected discipline from others and showed great self-discipline himself. However, under the stress of war he could become cruel towards his defeated enemies.

Source C

> Henry had no right to the crown of France. He had no right to that of England either. According to the legend, the war with France showed Henry's military genius. Really, it was a story of gambler's luck. The superior French army got stuck in the mud at Agincourt. At Agincourt, he was a war criminal, massacring prisoners in defiance of the conventions of war.

2. How far do **Sources B** and **C** disagree about the role of Henry V in the Hundred Years' War?   **4**

3. What part did Joan of Arc play in reawakening French national pride?   **5**

[END OF CONTEXT 3]

HISTORICAL STUDY: EUROPEAN AND WORLD

CONTEXT 4: NEW WORLDS: EUROPE IN THE AGE OF EXPANSION, 1480s–1530s

Answer the following questions using recalled knowledge and information from the sources where appropriate.

Source A is about shipbuilding and navigation.

Source A

> The Age of Exploration was possible because of new inventions. The most important of these inventions was the carrack. This ship had a lateen sail which made ships faster and far more manouverable. Longer journeys were possible which encouraged European rulers to search for new lands. Astrolabes helped sailors identify their location at sea. The development of log lines helped sailors calculate their speed and longitude. A great deal of expansion was then achieved in just fifty years.

1. Why did developments in shipbuilding and navigation make voyages of exploration easier between the 1480s and 1530s? (Use **Source A** and recall.)   **5**

Sources B and **C** describe Columbus's arrival in the New World.

Source B

> They arrived at a small island. Soon the local people came to watch them. The Admiral went on shore with Vicente Yanez, the captain of the Nina. The Admiral called to the two captains and to the others who leaped on shore, and said that they should bear faithful testimony that he had taken possession of the said island for the King and Queen. He presented the natives with red caps and strings of beads to wear upon the neck.

Source C

> After a voyage of more than two months the fleet sighted land. On 12th October Columbus set foot in the New World. Watched by naked, silent natives, he took control of the island in the name of the King and Queen of Spain and gave thanks to God. Gifts were exchanged with the natives. Columbus believed they were somewhere in the Indies, near Cipangu.

2. How far do **Sources B** and **C** agree about what happened when Christopher Columbus first arrived in the New World?   **4**

3. Describe the exploration of North America up to 1540.   **5**

[END OF CONTEXT 4]

Marks

HISTORICAL STUDY: EUROPEAN AND WORLD

CONTEXT 5: "TEA AND FREEDOM": THE AMERICAN REVOLUTION, 1763–1783

Answer the following questions using recalled knowledge and information from the sources where appropriate.

Source A is about the colonists' relationship with Britain.

Source A

> Many colonists were suffering as trade was poor and they believed the British government was responsible. Despite this, the Americans hoped that the economy would soon improve. However, Granville, a British government minister, introduced tough trade policies which made things worse. Consequently, the colonists saw British naval officers and customs men as greedy and unwanted. They represented a distant and unsympathetic government. This helped push many well-to-do colonists towards opposition to Britain and increased the likelihood of armed rebellion.

1. Why were many colonists unhappy with British rule by 1776? (Use **Source A** and recall.) **5**

Sources B and **C** are about the American forces which fought against the British army.

Source B

> The Revolutionary War was waged by small armies. The American forces were often led by inefficient, even incompetent, commanders who fought muddled campaigns. The men gathering in Boston were enthusiastic but badly armed and lacking supplies. The American commander, George Washington, could rely on no more than 5000 regular soldiers. Most men were part-time and served for only a few months. Britain's professional army was larger but not large enough to subdue the Americans.

Source C

> Many officers who led the American forces were not trained in the different types of warfare. The whole army was short of artillery, cavalry and almost all sorts of supplies. Within each state there were part-time soldiers. Many were militiamen who met and trained in their spare time and, although they did not have a uniform, they still came to fight for their country's freedom.

2. To what extent do **Sources B** and **C** agree about the condition of the American army? **4**
3. Describe the events leading up to the British surrender at Saratoga in 1777. **5**

[END OF CONTEXT 5]

HISTORICAL STUDY: EUROPEAN AND WORLD

CONTEXT 6: "THIS ACCURSED TRADE": THE BRITISH SLAVE TRADE AND ITS ABOLITION, 1770–1807

Answer the following questions using recalled knowledge and information from the sources where appropriate.

1. Describe conditions for slaves during the Middle Passage. **5**

Sources A and **B** describe slave auctions in the West Indies.

Source A

> Slaves were treated in most cases like cattle. A man went about the country buying up slaves and he was called a "speculator". Then he would sell them to the highest bidder. Oh! It was pitiful to see children taken from their mothers' breasts, mothers sold, husbands sold to a different owner than their wives. One woman had a baby and he wouldn't buy the baby.

Source B

> The slave master made us hold up our heads while customers felt our hands and arms and looked at our teeth, precisely as someone examines a horse which he is about to purchase. All the time the auction was going on one mother was crying aloud. She begged the man not to buy her son unless he also bought her; but the boy was sold on his own to the man who offered the most money.

2. How far do **Sources A** and **B** agree about what happened during slave auctions? **4**

Source C explains why people were in favour of the slave trade.

Source C

> The slave trade continued to be defended by businessmen who made large profits from it. Evidence from Bristol and Liverpool indicated that profits of 30 per cent from slave voyages were common. The Triangular Trade linked Britain, West Africa and the Caribbean. The Triangular Trade also helped Britain's industrial development. In Manchester, for example, it was said to have helped the growth in manufacturing. Work was provided for many at the port of Liverpool.

3. Why were some people in favour of the slave trade? (Use **Source C** and recall.) **5**

[END OF CONTEXT 6]

HISTORICAL STUDY: EUROPEAN AND WORLD

CONTEXT 7: CITIZENS! THE FRENCH REVOLUTION, 1789–1794

Answer the following questions using recalled knowledge and information from the sources where appropriate.

1. Describe the changes introduced by the Legislative Assembly in 1791. **5**

Source A describes the growth of feeling against the monarchy in France in 1792.

Source A

> Although Louis had been allowed to live comfortably in his palace he made no secret that he disliked having to share power with the Legislative Assembly. He supported war with Austria hoping that French defeat would restore his royal authority. The radicals imprisoned the king and his family after the storming of the Tuileries. Louis rejected the advice of moderate advisors to fully implement the Constitution of 1791. By then many people suspected that Louis was privately encouraging counter-revolution.

2. Why was there growing dislike of the monarchy in France in 1792? (Use **Source A** and recall.) **5**

Sources B and **C** describe the events of September 1792 which came to be known as the September Massacres.

Source B

> On August 10th 1792, Danton's supporters seized control and set up the Commune which became the real power in Paris. Danton gave a violent speech encouraging the Paris mobs to rise up. The sans-culottes attacked the prisons which they believed were secretly sheltering enemies of the revolution. They killed about one and a half thousand people. Street fights continued and barricades were set up all over the city.

Source C

> The news of the invasion of France by the Prussian army led to panic in Paris. Working class people began rioting, believing they were defending the revolution. From the night of September 2nd, in three prisons in Paris at least fifteen hundred women, priests and soldiers were brutally murdered. Although Danton condemned the massacres, he must take the blame for having stirred up the sans-culottes.

3. How far do **Sources B** and **C** agree about the events of the September Massacres in Paris in 1792? **4**

[END OF CONTEXT 7]

HISTORICAL STUDY: EUROPEAN AND WORLD

CONTEXT 8: CAVOUR, GARIBALDI AND THE MAKING OF ITALY, 1815–1870

Answer the following questions using recalled knowledge and information from the sources where appropriate.

1. Describe the growth of nationalism in Italy between 1815 and 1847. **5**

Sources A and **B** describe the events of the 1848 revolutions in Milan and Naples.

Source A

> Early in the year trouble broke out in Milan. The sight of Austrian soldiers smoking in the streets was an excuse for the people to show their dislike of the troops. Small-scale fights broke out, quickly followed by larger riots and eventually by a full scale revolution. The Austrian commander decided to withdraw his troops from the area. The revolutionaries set up a provisional government and prepared to continue the fight against Austria.

Source B

> There were clashes between the people and the troops in Naples. Arms were handed out to the townspeople and the next day protest grew as peasants from outside the city arrived to join the rising. The army replied by shelling the city and two days later reinforcements of 5000 troops arrived. Despite this, by April the revolutionaries had taken over. The middle and upper-class nationalists set up a provisional government.

2. How far do **Sources A** and **B** agree about the events of the 1848 revolutions in the Italian cities? **4**

Source C describes the importance of Garibaldi.

Source C

> As a military leader Garibaldi was a good, sometimes brilliant, commander, excellent at sizing up the situation. He inspired great enthusiasm and devotion in his men. His conquest of the south was a remarkable achievement. His chance meeting with Mazzini in 1833 gave him a cause to fight for. All Garibaldi's actions can be explained by his total devotion to the idea of Italian unity. It became the driving obsession of his life.

3. Why was Garibaldi important to the unification of Italy in 1861? (Use **Source C** and recall.) **5**

[END OF CONTEXT 8]

HISTORICAL STUDY: EUROPEAN AND WORLD

CONTEXT 9: IRON AND BLOOD? BISMARCK AND THE CREATION OF THE GERMAN EMPIRE, 1815–1871

Answer the following questions using recalled knowledge and information from the sources where appropriate.

Sources A and **B** describe actions against the student movement in Germany in the early nineteenth century.

Source A

> At a student demonstration an Austrian spy was murdered. The Austrian government was determined to prevent further incidents. At a meeting of the Confederation of Carlsbad in 1819, it was agreed to set up inspectors to oversee the universities. In addition to this, student organisations were outlawed. In most German states a strict press censorship was enforced. The effect of the decrees was the dismissal of a number of professors.

Source B

> The first sign of nationalist feeling occurred in the Students' Unions in the universities. Metternich and the Austrian government were determined to stop this. At a meeting of the Confederation at Carlsbad in 1819, decrees were passed which suppressed the student societies, causing many university teachers to be dismissed. Student societies re-emerged in the 1830s. Flags of black, red and gold came to symbolise liberal ideas.

1. How far do **Sources A** and **B** agree about the actions taken against the student movement? **4**

Source C is about the growth of nationalism in the German states.

Source C

> The folk tales of the Brothers Grimm celebrated Germany's past and looked forward to the day when it would at last be one nation. United by language, it was felt by many that the German states should also be united by the same government. By 1836, twenty five of the thirty nine German states had joined the Zollverein. The development of the railways in the 1830s and 1840s had made the German states co-operate, ending their isolation from one another. By 1850 over 3000 miles of railways had been laid.

2. Why did nationalism grow within the German states between 1815 and 1850? (Use **Source C** and recall.) **5**

3. Describe the events leading to Austria's defeat by Prussia in 1866. **5**

[END OF CONTEXT 9]

HISTORICAL STUDY: EUROPEAN AND WORLD

CONTEXT 10: THE RED FLAG: LENIN AND THE RUSSIAN REVOLUTION, 1894–1921

Answer the following questions using recalled knowledge and information from the sources where appropriate.

Source A is about the outbreak of the 1905 Revolution.

Source A

> By 1905 there was a growing desire to overthrow the repressive government of Nicholas II. There was a great deal of poverty in the cities and the countryside. The revolutionary movement gained strength following Russia's humiliating defeat by Japan. In January an uprising to remove the Tsar began. The non-Russian areas of the empire witnessed violent disturbances. Revolutionary groups became much more organised. They formed a soviet in St Petersburg. A soviet was a type of worker's parliament.

1. Why was there a revolution in Russia in 1905? (Use **Source A** and recall.)   5

2. Describe the effects of the First World War on the Russian people.   5

In **Sources B** and **C**, Bolshevik leaders argue about the decision to call a revolution in October 1917.

Source B is from a letter by Lenin.

Source B

> The Bolsheviks can and must take state power immediately into their own hands. They can do so because revolutionary elements in Petrograd and Moscow are now very strong. We can and must overcome our opponents' resistance and gain power. By promising peace and land we will be able to form a government that no-one will be able to overthrow. The majority of the people are on our side. By seizing power in Moscow and Petrograd we shall win absolutely and unquestionably.

Source C is from a letter by two Bolsheviks, Kamenev and Zinoviev.

Source C

> We are convinced that to call an uprising now would put the party and the revolution at risk. Our party is strong but the workers and soldiers are not ready to take to the streets now. The right mood does not exist. The party must be given time to grow. An uprising now will destroy what we have already achieved. We raise a voice against this ruinous policy.

3. How far do **Sources B** and **C** disagree about the decision to call a revolution in October 1917?   4

[END OF CONTEXT 10]

HISTORICAL STUDY: EUROPEAN AND WORLD

CONTEXT 11: FREE AT LAST? RACE RELATIONS IN THE USA, 1918–1968

Answer the following questions using recalled knowledge and information from the sources where appropriate.

1. What problems faced black Americans who moved north in the 1920s and 1930s? **5**

Source A explains black Americans' reaction to the Civil Rights Movement.

Source A

> Between 1945 and 1959, the Civil Rights Movement made much progress. Black activists, especially the NAACP, were the moving force behind Supreme Court decisions. The Supreme Court had declared segregated schools unconstitutional in 1954. Progress in carrying out this declaration was very slow over the next ten years. Unending black pressure forced President Eisenhower to propose a Civil Rights Act in 1957. The Civil Rights Movement was gaining heroes such as Rosa Parks during this period, though there were also victims such as Emmett Till.

2. Why did black Americans feel that progress towards civil rights had been made between 1945 and 1959? (Use **Source A** and recall.) **5**

Sources B and **C** describe the sit-ins.

Source B

> Some Civil Rights workers believed that the sit-ins showed students that they could take action themselves. Young black people realised that they could make a difference to Civil Rights by winning the support of both black and white Americans. However, sit-ins only achieved limited success in some of the towns and cities where the protests were used. Much more needed to be done to improve Civil Rights.

Source C

> The very act of protesting meant the students believed they could make a difference. When they "sat in" these young people practiced non-violence, they dressed in their best clothes and they studied books. This helped to encourage black community support and won the respect and even admiration of some white Americans. However, the sit-ins only enjoyed success in a few Southern states. In the Deep South, white Americans refused to desegregate and the protestors faced resistance from the white authorities.

3. How far do **Sources B** and **C** agree about the success of the sit-ins? **4**

[END OF CONTEXT 11]

HISTORICAL STUDY: EUROPEAN AND WORLD

CONTEXT 12: THE ROAD TO WAR, 1933–1939

Answer the following questions using recalled knowledge and information from the sources where appropriate.

Source A is about Britain's policy of Appeasement in the 1930s.

Source A

> The Great Depression meant that money could not be found for rearmament and the government knew that the British people were totally opposed to war. Chamberlain, who had been Chancellor before becoming Prime Minister in 1937, had a reputation as a social reformer. Chamberlain was in favour of personal, face to face talks among Europe's leaders and believed he could negotiate directly with Hitler. The British Government took the view that communist Russia was the real threat to peace in the world.

1. Why did Britain follow a policy of Appeasement in the 1930s? (Use **Source A** and recall.) 5

2. Describe the aims of Hitler's foreign policy. 5

Sources B and **C** are opinions about the Anschluss between Germany and Austria in 1938.

Source B

> It is clear that Anschluss is popular among the Austrian people who are, after all, German in language and culture. Keeping Germany and Austria apart had been one of the more spiteful terms of Versailles and this wrong is now made right. Therefore Europe is likely to benefit from a period of peace and prosperity as Germany moves into a brighter future.

Source C

> Germany has taken over Austria. Any intelligent person can see that an even more powerful Germany is a threat to the peace and stability of Europe. The decision in 1919 to forbid Anschluss had been a very sensible one for limiting the war-like ambitions of Germany. We have permitted Hitler to brutally invade an independent country whose population has no love for Nazism.

3. How far do **Sources B** and **C** disagree about the Anschluss? 4

[END OF CONTEXT 12]

HISTORICAL STUDY: EUROPEAN AND WORLD

CONTEXT 13: IN THE SHADOW OF THE BOMB: THE COLD WAR, 1945–1985

Marks

Answer the following questions using recalled knowledge and information from the sources where appropriate.

Source A is about the Berlin Wall.

Source A

> On 12 August 1961 a record 4000 East Germans fled to West Berlin to start a new life in the West. Those who left were often young and well educated. In the small hours of 13 August, Soviet and East German "shock workers" closed the border and put barbed wire across the streets. The East Germans claimed that enemy agents had been stationed in West Berlin. The agents were using Berlin as a centre of operations against East Germany and the Soviet Union. Berlin had become a divided city.

1. Why did the Soviet Union build the Berlin Wall in 1961? (Use **Source A** and recall.) — 5

Sources B and **C** are about the tactics of the Vietcong.

Source B

> The Vietcong, or "Charlie" as the Americans called them, were the locally born guerrilla fighters of South Vietnam. The Vietcong consisted of three groups: units of regular soldiers, provincial forces, and part-time guerrillas. The Vietcong generally avoided large scale attacks on the enemy but continually harassed their troops and installations causing heavy American casualties. They travelled light, carrying basic weapons and few supplies.

Source C

> Our first real battle was in the Michelin Rubber Plantation. Thousands of Vietcong launched wave after wave of attacks on our camp. But they had all kinds of Chinese and Russian weapons, such as flamethrowers and rocket launchers. Eventually we counter-attacked and pushed them back. Fortunately, we only lost around seven guys. The Vietcong body count was reported to have been 800, but I thought it was more.

2. How far do **Sources B** and **C** disagree about the tactics used by the Vietcong? — 4

3. Describe the steps taken to reduce tension between the USA and the USSR during the 1960s and 1970s. — 5

[END OF CONTEXT 13]

[END OF PART 3: EUROPEAN AND WORLD CONTEXTS]

[END OF QUESTION PAPER]

[BLANK PAGE]

INTERMEDIATE 2
2010

[BLANK PAGE]

X044/201

NATIONAL QUALIFICATIONS 2010

WEDNESDAY, 26 MAY 9.00 AM – 10.45 AM

HISTORY INTERMEDIATE 2

The instructions for this paper are on *Page two*. Read them carefully before you begin your answers. Your Invigilator will tell you which contexts to answer in Parts 2 and 3 of the examination.

INSTRUCTIONS

Answer **one** question from Part 1, The Short Essay

Answer **one** context* from Part 2, Scottish and British

Answer **one** context* from Part 3, European and World

Answer **one** other context* from

    either   Part 2, Scottish and British

    or   Part 3, European and World

*Answer all the questions in each of your chosen contexts.

Contents

Part 1 Short Essay Questions.
Answer **one** question only. Pages 4–6

Part 2 Scottish and British Contexts

1. Murder in the Cathedral: Crown, Church and People, 1154–1173 — Page 8
2. Wallace, Bruce and the Wars of Independence, 1286–1328 — Page 9
3. Mary, Queen of Scots and the Scottish Reformation, 1540s–1587 — Page 10
4. The Coming of the Civil War, 1603–1642 — Page 11
5. "Ane End of Ane Auld Sang": Scotland and the Treaty of Union, 1690s–1715 — Page 12
6. Immigrants and Exiles: Scotland, 1830s–1930s — Page 13
7. From the Cradle to the Grave? Social Welfare in Britain, 1890s–1951 — Page 14
8. Campaigning for Change: Social Change in Scotland, 1900s–1979 — Page 15
9. A Time of Troubles: Ireland, 1900–1923 — Page 16

Part 3 European and World Contexts

1. The Norman Conquest, 1060–1153 — Page 17
2. The Cross and the Crescent: The First Crusade, 1096–1125 — Page 18
3. War, Death and Revolt in Medieval Europe, 1328–1436 — Page 19
4. New Worlds: Europe in the Age of Expansion, 1480s–1530s — Page 20
5. "Tea and Freedom": The American Revolution, 1763–1783 — Page 21
6. "This Accursed Trade": The British Slave Trade and its Abolition, 1770–1807 — Page 22
7. Citizens! The French Revolution, 1789–1794 — Page 23
8. Cavour, Garibaldi and the Making of Italy, 1815–1870 — Page 24
9. Iron and Blood? Bismarck and the Creation of the German Empire, 1815–1871 — Page 25
10. The Red Flag: Lenin and the Russian Revolution, 1894–1921 — Page 26
11. Free at Last? Race Relations in the USA, 1918–1968 — Page 27
12. The Road to War, 1933–1939 — Page 28
13. In the Shadow of the Bomb: The Cold War, 1945–1985 — Page 29

[Turn over

PART 1: THE SHORT ESSAY

Answer **one** question. For this question you should write a short essay using your own knowledge. The essay should include an introduction, development and conclusion. Each question is worth 8 marks.

SCOTTISH AND BRITISH CONTEXTS:

CONTEXT 1: MURDER IN THE CATHEDRAL: CROWN, CHURCH AND PEOPLE, 1154–1173

Question 1: Explain why Henry II faced difficulties on becoming king in 1154.   8

CONTEXT 2: WALLACE, BRUCE AND THE WARS OF INDEPENDENCE, 1286–1328

Question 2: Explain why the Scots won the battle at Bannockburn.   8

CONTEXT 3: MARY, QUEEN OF SCOTS AND THE SCOTTISH REFORMATION, 1540s–1587

Question 3: Explain why Riccio became unpopular with Darnley and the Scottish nobles.   8

CONTEXT 4: THE COMING OF THE CIVIL WAR, 1603–1642

Question 4: Explain why Charles I was an unpopular monarch in England by 1640.   8

CONTEXT 5: "ANE END OF ANE AULD SANG": SCOTLAND AND THE TREATY OF UNION, 1690s–1715

Question 5: Explain why many Scots were disappointed by the Act of Union by 1715.   8

CONTEXT 6: IMMIGRANTS AND EXILES: SCOTLAND, 1830s–1930s

Question 6: Explain why Irish immigrants were attracted to Scotland between 1830 and 1930.   8

CONTEXT 7: FROM THE CRADLE TO THE GRAVE? SOCIAL WELFARE IN BRITAIN, 1890s–1951

Question 7: Explain why the Liberal government passed social welfare reforms between 1906 and 1914.   8

Marks

CONTEXT 8: CAMPAIGNING FOR CHANGE: SOCIAL CHANGE IN SCOTLAND, 1900s–1979

Question 8: Explain why there was still a need to improve many women's lives after 1918. **8**

CONTEXT 9: A TIME OF TROUBLES: IRELAND, 1900–1923

Question 9: Explain why the Anglo-Irish War broke out in 1919. **8**

EUROPEAN AND WORLD CONTEXTS:

CONTEXT 1: THE NORMAN CONQUEST, 1060–1153

Question 10: Explain why knights were important in medieval society. **8**

CONTEXT 2: THE CROSS AND THE CRESCENT: THE FIRST CRUSADE, 1096–1125

Question 11: Explain why the Crusaders were able to keep control of the Holy Land after 1097. **8**

CONTEXT 3: WAR, DEATH AND REVOLT IN MEDIEVAL EUROPE, 1328–1436

Question 12: Explain why France was unsuccessful in the war against England between 1415 and 1422. **8**

CONTEXT 4: NEW WORLDS: EUROPE IN THE AGE OF EXPANSION, 1480s–1530s

Question 13: Explain why the Spaniards were able to defeat **either** the Aztecs **or** the Incas. **8**

CONTEXT 5: "TEA AND FREEDOM": THE AMERICAN REVOLUTION, 1763–1783

Question 14: Explain why the American War of Independence broke out in 1775. **8**

CONTEXT 6: "THIS ACCURSED TRADE": THE BRITISH SLAVE TRADE AND ITS ABOLITION, 1770–1807

Question 15: Explain why it took so long for Britain to abolish the slave trade. **8**

[Turn over

CONTEXT 7: CITIZENS! THE FRENCH REVOLUTION, 1789–1794

Question 16: Explain why the French people were unhappy with their government by 1789. **8**

CONTEXT 8: CAVOUR, GARIBALDI AND THE MAKING OF ITALY, 1815–1870

Question 17: Explain why Garibaldi's leadership was important to the unification of Italy. **8**

CONTEXT 9: IRON AND BLOOD? BISMARCK AND THE CREATION OF THE GERMAN EMPIRE, 1815–1871

Question 18: Explain why the nationalist movement had failed to unite the German states by 1850. **8**

CONTEXT 10: THE RED FLAG: LENIN AND THE RUSSIAN REVOLUTION, 1894–1921

Question 19: Explain why the Tsar was able to remain in power following the 1905 revolution. **8**

CONTEXT 11: FREE AT LAST? RACE RELATIONS IN THE USA, 1918–1968

Question 20: Explain why the demand for civil rights continued to grow after 1945. **8**

CONTEXT 12: THE ROAD TO WAR, 1933–1939

Question 21: Explain why Hitler's actions created problems in Europe between 1933 and 1939. **8**

CONTEXT 13: IN THE SHADOW OF THE BOMB: THE COLD WAR, 1945–1985

Question 22: Explain why America lost the war in Vietnam. **8**

[END OF PART 1: THE SHORT ESSAY]

[Turn over for PART 2: SCOTTISH AND BRITISH CONTEXTS on *Page eight*

PART 2:

HISTORICAL STUDY: SCOTTISH AND BRITISH

CONTEXT 1: MURDER IN THE CATHEDRAL: CROWN, CHURCH AND PEOPLE, 1154–1173

Answer the following questions using recalled knowledge and information from the sources where appropriate.

Source A explains why castles were important in the twelfth century.

Source A

> During Henry II's reign, castles were built of stone and with extra walls and towers. These castles became a key symbol of power. They were also the administrative centres of each town. The numerous rooms inside a castle meant that it was an ideal base for the local garrison carrying out guard duty. Although many castles had been built illegally during the civil war there was no doubt that they were useful during times of attack when food, drink and other supplies could be stored there.

1. Why were castles important in the twelfth century? (Use **Source A** and recall.) 5

Sources B and **C** describe the life of a monk in medieval times.

Source B

> At 2 o'clock in the morning, monks were woken for a service in the chapel. Although they were given time to sleep, monks were expected to pray at least 8 times a day. Breakfast included bread and fruit and was eaten in silence. After breakfast, monks were allowed a little free time but were expected to spend most of the day working in the fields or carrying out other duties.

Source C

> Many monks lived their lives by St Benedict's rule. During meal times talking was strictly forbidden so monks listened to prayers or to readings from holy books. Services began in the middle of the night and every monk was expected to pray in church several times a day. Isolated from the local community, monks were not allowed to leave the monastery and had to forget their previous life.

2. How far do **Sources B** and **C** agree about the lives of monks in medieval times? 4

3. Describe the murder of Archbishop Becket. 5

[END OF CONTEXT 1]

HISTORICAL STUDY: SCOTTISH AND BRITISH

CONTEXT 2: WALLACE, BRUCE AND THE WARS OF INDEPENDENCE, 1286–1328

Answer the following questions using recalled knowledge and information from the sources where appropriate.

1. Describe the events between 1286 and 1292 that led to Edward I becoming overlord of Scotland. **5**

Source A explains why the leadership of William Wallace was important.

Source A

> Wallace has become a folk hero in Scotland. Although he was only the second son of an unimportant knight, for a short while he became Guardian of Scotland uniting people under his leadership. He reorganised the army of Scotland and prepared for an English invasion. He also looked for foreign help. Bishop Lamberton was sent to Rome and Paris to plead Scotland's cause there. Wallace also renewed trade with Germany to obtain iron for weapons which he needed for his army.

2. Why was the leadership of William Wallace important during the Wars of Independence? (Use **Source A** and recall.) **5**

Sources B and **C** are about the amount of support Robert Bruce had in 1320.

Source B

> In the Declaration of Arbroath of 1320, the Scottish nobles explained to the Pope why all the Scots thought Robert Bruce was their king. They argued that he had royal blood and that his actions had won him the support of the Scottish people. On top of that, they argued that they wanted him as king because he had saved Scotland from being taken over by the King of England.

Source C

> Even while the Declaration of Arbroath was being written, some Scottish nobles were plotting against Robert Bruce. They felt he was a ruthless thug who had murdered his main rival in a church. Other Scottish nobles claimed to be more closely related to the Scottish royal family than Bruce. They, however, had not been successful in war. These disagreements caused problems in Scotland.

3. How far do **Sources B** and **C** disagree about the amount of support Robert Bruce had in 1320? **4**

[END OF CONTEXT 2]

HISTORICAL STUDY: SCOTTISH AND BRITISH

CONTEXT 3: MARY, QUEEN OF SCOTS AND THE SCOTTISH REFORMATION, 1540s–1587

Answer the following questions using recalled knowledge and information from the sources where appropriate.

Source A explains why Henry VIII ordered the invasions of Scotland after 1544.

Source A

> The death of King James V after the Scottish defeat at Solway Moss gave King Henry VIII the opportunity to break the Auld Alliance between France and Scotland. He freed Scottish prisoners of war on condition they supported the marriage of Mary to his son, Edward. Within a year the Scots had agreed to this in the Treaty of Greenwich. However, when Henry then made more and more demands on them, the French encouraged the Scots to resist. Finally the Scots announced that the Treaty was broken.

1. Why did Henry VIII of England order the invasions of Scotland after 1544? (Use **Source A** and recall.) 5

2. Describe the events leading up to the signing of the Treaty of Edinburgh in 1560. 5

Sources B and **C** are about how well Mary, Queen of Scots ruled Scotland.

Source B

> Mary returned to Scotland as Queen in 1561. Mary was a Roman Catholic who believed that she should rule England instead of her Protestant cousin, Elizabeth. She neglected the government of Scotland by leaving the running of the country to a group of Protestant nobles. She did not really care about the issue of religion in Scotland.

Source C

> Until Mary allowed her heart to rule her head by marrying Darnley, she had been a successful ruler in Scotland. She had defeated the nobles who challenged her authority and had established a successful government under her half-brother Moray. As a Roman Catholic, her tolerant treatment of Scotland's new Protestant church was ahead of its time.

3. How far do **Sources B** and **C** disagree about how well Mary, Queen of Scots ruled Scotland? 4

[END OF CONTEXT 3]

HISTORICAL STUDY: SCOTTISH AND BRITISH

CONTEXT 4: THE COMING OF THE CIVIL WAR, 1603–1642

Answer the following questions using recalled knowledge and information from the sources where appropriate.

Sources A and **B** describe James VI and I.

Source A

> James VI and I was well educated and clever. The Union of the Crowns united the monarchs of Scotland and England and James became king of both countries. He claimed that kings were appointed by God, and could do as they wished. He lost people's respect by giving money and power to favourites at court. His son, Charles I was to prove a less popular king.

Source B

> The reign of the Stuarts began in 1603. James VI and I was a highly intelligent man. From the start of his reign he spent a lot of money, not only on himself but on gifts and pensions to courtiers. Although he believed in the Divine Right of Kings he did not try to be an absolute monarch in his relations with Parliament. Charles I would use his royal prerogative to a greater extent.

1. How far do **Sources A** and **B** agree about James VI and I? **4**

2. Describe the methods used by James VI and I to raise money during his reign. **5**

Source C explains why Charles I faced opposition to his rule in Scotland.

Source C

> When Charles decided to enforce his religious views on the Scottish people, he met fierce resistance. Many Scots were Presbyterians who carried out their own religious services and they disliked these changes. They showed this when they signed the National Covenant in 1638, sometimes in blood. The Scots also resented Charles because he was an absentee King and he visited Scotland only once during his reign. Scotland was a poor country and many Scots thought Charles did not care. Deep resentment and suspicion grew across Scotland.

3. Why did Charles I face opposition to his rule in Scotland? (Use **Source C** and recall.) **5**

[END OF CONTEXT 4]

HISTORICAL STUDY: SCOTTISH AND BRITISH

CONTEXT 5: "ANE END OF ANE AULD SANG": SCOTLAND AND THE TREATY OF UNION, 1690s–1715

Answer the following questions using recalled knowledge and information from the sources where appropriate.

1. Describe what happened during the Worcester affair. **5**

Source A explains why Queen Anne wanted a Treaty of Union.

Source A

> Queen Anne came to the throne of Scotland and England in 1702. She wanted a complete Union of the two countries because she found it difficult to control the Scottish Parliament. She also faced complaints that her policies were harming Scotland. The Scottish Parliament was even threatening to end the Union of the Crowns. However, at first, these problems with Scotland made it more difficult for England to fight the war against France.

2. Why did Queen Anne want a Treaty of Union between England and Scotland? (Use **Source A** and recall.) **5**

Sources B and **C** are about Scottish attitudes to the Treaty of Union.

Source B

> The Treaty of Union was passed in 1707. Scots thought the Equivalent was money to help the country recover from the Darien Scheme. Scots felt they would have influence in a new and more powerful kingdom. They thought their traders would benefit from access to English colonies.

Source C

> Scots feared that, once they lost their independence, they would have little influence over government decisions. Others worried that businesses in Scotland would suffer from competition from English imports. They also thought the money paid to Scotland was a bribe to rich and powerful men—the only way that a Union could be passed.

3. How far do **Sources B** and **C** disagree about Scottish attitudes to the Treaty of Union? **4**

[END OF CONTEXT 5]

HISTORICAL STUDY: SCOTTISH AND BRITISH

CONTEXT 6: IMMIGRANTS AND EXILES: SCOTLAND, 1830s–1930s

Answer the following questions using recalled knowledge and information from the sources where appropriate.

Sources A and **B** are about Scottish attitudes to Irish immigration.

Source A

> Irish immigrants tended to concentrate in particular areas because they were disliked by the native Scots. It was natural that the immigrants should live together but the determination to stick to their own culture was looked upon with suspicion. There were accusations that they did not wish to become "new Scots". In addition, the Irish did not receive much credit for their contribution to the Scottish economy.

Source B

> There was a reluctance to admit that Irish workers were essential to the development of industry in Scotland even though they were to be found wherever work needed doing. Many Scots criticised immigrants for keeping to their native language and religion. It became clear that there was a great deal of resentment against the immigrants in Scotland.

1. How far do **Sources A** and **B** agree about Scottish attitudes to Irish immigration? **4**

Source C explains why poor Scots were able to emigrate in the nineteenth century.

Source C

> Some landlords saw it as in their own interests to encourage poor tenants to seek their fortunes elsewhere. The landlords were willing to pay the full travelling costs, especially to Canada. Landlords often wrote off rent arrears so that the tenants would have some money for their new life and some even bought their cattle which provided the emigrant with some extra help. Glasgow and Edinburgh feared a massive influx of Highlanders and the city authorities made a contribution towards their expenses in emigrating.

2. Why were many poor Scots able to emigrate during the nineteenth century? (Use **Source C** and recall.) **5**

3. In what ways did Scots help to improve the lands to which they emigrated? **5**

[END OF CONTEXT 6]

HISTORICAL STUDY: SCOTTISH AND BRITISH

CONTEXT 7: FROM THE CRADLE TO THE GRAVE? SOCIAL WELFARE IN BRITAIN, 1890s–1951

Answer the following questions using recalled knowledge and information from the sources where appropriate.

Sources A and **B** describe the Old Age Pensions Act of 1908.

Source A

> The Liberal government passed a series of welfare reforms to help the old, the young and the sick. A pensioner with a yearly income of up to £21 received the full 25p a week. Pensions were not made available to those who had been in prison during the previous ten years. The pension was not a generous amount. The Liberals were criticised for not doing enough to tackle the real causes of poverty.

Source B

> The Pensions Act entitled people over seventy with an annual income of up to £21 to 25p a week of a pension. The government stated that these payments were not meant to be a complete solution to the problem of poverty in old age. However, the foundation stones of the welfare state had been laid. Any seventy year old was entitled to a pension provided they had avoided imprisonment in the previous ten years and they had not continually avoided work.

1. How far do **Sources A** and **B** agree about the Old Age Pensions Act of 1908? **4**

2. Describe the ways the Beveridge Report of 1942 suggested tackling the social problems facing Britain. **5**

Source C is about the welfare reforms passed by the Labour government between 1945 and 1951.

Source C

> Poor housing and homelessness were still serious problems by 1951. The Labour government also did little to enhance the educational opportunities for working class children, most of whom left school at fifteen with no paper qualifications. People thought the National Health Service was a great success but there was still a shortage of hospitals and health centres. There was still a long way to go before the problems of poverty and deprivation were adequately solved. The Labour Party lost the General Election of 1951.

3. Why were some people disappointed with the Labour welfare reforms by 1951? (Use **Source C** and recall.) **5**

[END OF CONTEXT 7]

HISTORICAL STUDY: SCOTTISH AND BRITISH

CONTEXT 8: CAMPAIGNING FOR CHANGE: SOCIAL CHANGE IN SCOTLAND, 1900s–1979

Answer the following questions using recalled knowledge and information from the sources where appropriate.

Sources A and **B** describe changes to Scots drinking habits in the early twentieth century.

Source A

> By 1900, people were drinking less alcohol. The number of public houses decreased and convictions for drunkenness fell. This was due more to the increased tax on alcohol than to the temperance movement. People also preferred to spend their money on the new consumer and household goods which were increasingly available, as well as on leisure activities.

Source B

> As the twentieth century progressed Scottish men were drinking much less than they had in the nineteenth century. The reasons for this are many. One was the development of many different things to do. The number of pubs in some areas fell where people voted for this. Alcohol became much more expensive when the government raised the tax on spirits by 34% in 1909 and then cut pub opening times to five and a half hours a day in 1914.

1. How far do **Sources A** and **B** agree about reasons why people were drinking less in Scotland in the early 20th century? **4**

2. Describe the unrest on Red Clydeside between 1915 and 1919. **5**

Source C describes the effects of North Sea Oil on the north of Scotland.

Source C

> Oil had a huge impact upon the north of Scotland. Aberdeen became the oil capital of Europe and the boom spread to smaller east coast towns such as Fraserburgh, Peterhead and Montrose. Giant rigs became a common sight in the Moray and Cromarty Firths because of the construction yards at Ardersier and Nigg. There were almost 3,000 new jobs created in the Shetland Islands. Dozens of companies moved to the north east to provide support and other services to the industry.

3. Why was the development of North Sea Oil so important for the economy of the north of Scotland? (Use **Source C** and recall.) **5**

[END OF CONTEXT 8]

HISTORICAL STUDY: SCOTTISH AND BRITISH

CONTEXT 9: A TIME OF TROUBLES: IRELAND, 1900–1923

Answer the following questions using recalled knowledge and information from the sources where appropriate.

Sources A and **B** are two Irish opinions on the Union with Britain.

Source A

> The Irish people have benefited greatly from the Union. We are better housed, fed and receive better wages for our work. Our freedom and rights have been protected and this has led to great success. In the past Ireland was a poor country with little or no future. Today Ireland works in partnership with Britain. It would be a disaster to listen to those who want to destroy all that Ireland has achieved.

Source B

> Until Ireland has the right to make its own laws we will have no freedom. For years we have been the losers in the Union with Britain. Although the Union is against the wishes of the people, the British are unwilling to listen. Unemployment and poor wages have made many Irish men and women desperate yet the British government does nothing to help. Conditions are so bad, Irish families are being forced to emigrate abroad in an attempt to try and improve their lives.

1. How far do **Sources A** and **B** disagree about the Union? **4**

2. Describe the actions taken by the Unionists against the Home Rule Bill. **5**

Source C explains why De Valera opposed the 1921 Treaty.

Source C

> After months of negotiations the Irish delegation in London reluctantly signed the 1921 Treaty. De Valera had remained in Dublin and was furious that terms had been agreed without consulting him. He refused to accept that six counties in the north of Ireland would be separated from the rest of the country. He also refused to swear an oath of allegiance to the British King. Although most people in Ireland wanted an end to the war, De Valera argued that only full independence would lead to peace.

3. Why did De Valera oppose the 1921 Treaty? (Use **Source C** and recall.) **5**

[END OF CONTEXT 9]

[END OF PART 2: SCOTTISH AND BRITISH CONTEXTS]

Marks

PART 3:

HISTORICAL STUDY: EUROPEAN AND WORLD

CONTEXT 1: THE NORMAN CONQUEST, 1060–1153

Answer the following questions using recalled knowledge and information from the sources where appropriate.

Source A is about the events leading up to the Battle of Hastings.

Source A

> William arrived at Pevensey with a huge army. He had countless horsemen and archers. When it was reported that William had landed, Harold at once forced his exhausted army to march south. Although he knew that some of the bravest of the Saxons had fallen in the two previous battles he advanced with full speed into the south of England. On 14 October Harold fought with the Normans nine miles from Hastings. However some of his soldiers refused to remain loyal to him and deserted from his army.

1. Why did Harold lose the battle of Hastings? (Use **Source A** and recall.) — **5**

Source B describes how William gained control of England after the Battle of Hastings. It was written by his priest in 1077.

Source B

> William went to various parts of his kingdom. He tried to organise everything to suit his people as well as himself. Wherever he went the people surrendered to him. There was no resistance, but everywhere men submitted to him and asked for his peace. He gave rich fiefs to the men he had brought over from France but no Frenchman was given anything that had been unjustly taken from an Englishman.

2. How useful is **Source B** as evidence about William's attempts to control England after 1066? — **4**

3. In what ways did Scotland change during the reign of David I? — **5**

[END OF CONTEXT 1]

HISTORICAL STUDY: EUROPEAN AND WORLD

CONTEXT 2: THE CROSS AND THE CRESCENT: THE FIRST CRUSADE, 1096–1125

Answer the following questions using recalled knowledge and information from the sources where appropriate.

Source A explains why Pope Urban II called the First Crusade.

Source A

> In 1095 Emperor Alexius sent messages to the Pope begging him for help against the Turks. Although Urban II had not been Pope for very long, he could see that the Turks were a threat to Christianity. Eight months later the Pope delivered a successful speech at Clermont. Almost immediately peasants and knights left their homes and took the cross. The Pope hoped the Crusade would stop western knights fighting amongst themselves and encourage them to recapture Jerusalem from the Turks.

1. Why did Pope Urban II call the First Crusade? (Use **Source A** and recall.)   **5**

2. Describe the siege and capture of Antioch by the First Crusade.   **5**

Source B describes the behaviour of the Crusaders at Marrat au Numan. It was written by a priest who went on the First Crusade.

Source B

> Although many knights stayed in Antioch or returned home, the main Crusading army continued the journey to Jerusalem. On the way we stayed at Marrat au Numan. Our men were starving and desperate for food. Some Crusaders began to rip up the bodies of their dead enemies. They cut their flesh into slices, cooked and ate them. Many of us were shocked by what we saw and could not wait to leave.

3. How useful is **Source B** as evidence of the Crusaders' behaviour in the Holy Land?   **4**

[END OF CONTEXT 2]

Marks

HISTORICAL STUDY: EUROPEAN AND WORLD

CONTEXT 3: WAR, DEATH AND REVOLT IN MEDIEVAL EUROPE, 1328–1436

Answer the following questions using recalled knowledge and information from the sources where appropriate.

1. Describe the problem of succession to the French throne after 1328. **5**

Source A is about the effects of the Battle of Poitiers on France. It was written by Froissart the chronicler in 1388.

Source A

> The battle was fought on the 19th day of September 1356. The finest knights of France died on that day. This severely weakened the realm of France. The country fell into great misery. In all, 17 lords were taken prisoner. Between 500 and 700 men-at-arms were killed. In all, 6,000 Frenchmen died.

2. How useful is **Source A** as evidence of the effects of the Battle of Poitiers on France? **4**

Source B is about the end of the Peasants' Revolt.

Source B

> The King was determined that the revolt would not succeed. He sent out his messengers to capture those who had led the revolt. Many were hanged. Gallows were set up all around the city of London and in other cities and boroughs to put people off joining in the revolt. At last the King, seeing that too many of his subjects would die, took pity. He granted pardons to some of the troublemakers on condition that they should never rebel again on pain of losing their lives. So this wicked revolt ended.

3. Why was the King able to crush the Peasants' Revolt? (Use **Source B** and recall.) **5**

[END OF CONTEXT 3]

HISTORICAL STUDY: EUROPEAN AND WORLD

CONTEXT 4: NEW WORLDS: EUROPE IN THE AGE OF EXPANSION, 1480s–1530s

Answer the following questions using recalled knowledge and information from the sources where appropriate.

Source A is from a letter by Columbus to a friend of Queen Isabella, written in 1500.

Source A

> I was sent as a captain from Spain to the Indies to conquer a large and warlike people, who had customs and beliefs very different from ours. These people live in mountains and forest without any settled townships. Here by God's will I have brought this new world under the dominion of Spain. By doing this, Spain, which was thought of by some people as poor, has now become rich.

1. How useful is **Source A** as evidence of reasons for European exploration between 1480 and 1530? **4**

2. In what ways did Vasco da Gama's voyage benefit Europe? **5**

Source B explains some of the problems faced by Magellan on his voyage round the world.

Source B

> Magellan left Seville with five ships full of goods to trade in the east. As a Portuguese captain commanding a Spanish fleet he was unpopular. He kept the destination secret so that the crew would not be afraid but this made him seem untrustworthy. In Patagonia the other captains plotted a mutiny against him. He crushed this and brutally executed the ringleaders. Further south, his ships had to pass through a stormy narrow straight which now bears his name. Two of his ships were lost there.

3. Why did Magellan face difficulties during his voyage round the world? (Use **Source B** and recall.) **5**

[END OF CONTEXT 4]

HISTORICAL STUDY: EUROPEAN AND WORLD

CONTEXT 5: "TEA AND FREEDOM": THE AMERICAN REVOLUTION, 1763–1783

Answer the following questions using recalled knowledge and information from the sources where appropriate.

1. Describe the Boston Tea Party and the British government's response to it.   **5**

Source A is from a letter written by the leaders of the 13 colonies when they met in May 1775.

Source A

> On the 19th day of April, General Gage sent out a large detachment of his army who made an unprovoked attack on the inhabitants of the town of Lexington. They murdered eight of the inhabitants and wounded many others. The troops then proceeded to the town of Concord, where they cruelly slaughtered several people and wounded many more, until they were forced to retreat by a group of brave colonists suddenly assembled to repel this cruel aggression.

2. How useful is **Source A** as evidence about what happened at Lexington and Concord in April 1775?   **4**

Source B explains the effects of the involvement of foreign countries in the American War of Independence.

Source B

> Representatives of America and France signed an alliance on 6 February 1778. The entry of France into the war added enormously to Britain's difficulties. The French attacked Britain's colonies in the Caribbean and elsewhere undermining Britain's control. They harassed British shipping in the Atlantic interfering with Britain's trade. Spain and the Netherlands had joined the anti-British alliance by 1780. As a result, Britain lost control of the seas for the first time that century. It became ever more difficult for Britain to reinforce and supply its forces in America.

3. Why did the involvement of foreign countries cause difficulties for Britain in the War of Independence? (Use **Source B** and recall.)   **5**

[END OF CONTEXT 5]

HISTORICAL STUDY: EUROPEAN AND WORLD

CONTEXT 6: "THIS ACCURSED TRADE": THE BRITISH SLAVE TRADE AND ITS ABOLITION, 1770–1807

Answer the following questions using recalled knowledge and information from the sources where appropriate.

1. Describe the different stages of the triangular trade. **5**

In **Source A**, a modern historian describes slave revolts in the West Indies.

Source A

> The British needed all the military help they could get in the 1790s when they faced slave unrest in Dominica, St Lucia, St Vincent and Grenada. Their greatest concern was for Jamaica, which was the biggest, the richest and most troublesome of their slave colonies. By the early nineteenth century, the island was undergoing what seemed like an endless series of revolts. In one of the worst rebellions, 226 properties were damaged at a cost estimated to be £1 million.

2. How useful is **Source A** as evidence of slave resistance in the West Indies? **4**

Source B explains why the slave trade was abolished in Britain.

Source B

> During the late nineteenth century, attitudes towards the slave trade were changing. More people began to think of Africans as fellow human beings and felt that they should be treated as such. Britain's trading interests were also changing. Trade with India and East Asia was growing while trade with the West Indies had become less important to Britain. Many merchants supported free trade. They argued that slavery was an inefficient way to produce sugar. In 1807, a new law made it illegal for British people to buy slaves in Africa.

3. Why was the slave trade abolished by Britain in 1807? (Use **Source B** and recall.) **5**

[END OF CONTEXT 6]

HISTORICAL STUDY: EUROPEAN AND WORLD

CONTEXT 7: CITIZENS! THE FRENCH REVOLUTION, 1789–1794

Answer the following questions using recalled knowledge and information from the sources where appropriate.

Source A is from the Tennis Court Oath agreed by the Third Estate in June 1789.

Source A

> Wherever the members of the Third Estate choose to meet, that is legally the National Assembly. No one has the right to prevent the members of the Assembly from gathering together when they want to. The National Assembly has the task of writing the constitution of France and to restore public order.

1. How useful is **Source A** as evidence of the relationship between the Third Estate and the King in June 1789? **4**

Source B explains why France was at war with other European countries after 1791.

Source B

> Austria and Prussia went to war because they objected to the way that Marie Antoinette, an Austrian Princess, was being treated. Louis XVI also wanted war but only because he secretly hoped that a French defeat would mean an end to the Revolution. On the other hand the revolutionaries wanted to spread their ideas throughout Europe. Only some of the radical Jacobins opposed war, preferring to consolidate and expand the Revolution at home. Britain joined the war against France to prevent the French interfering in other countries.

2. Why did war break out between France and her neighbours after 1791? (Use **Source B** and recall.) **5**

3. Describe the Reign of Terror. **5**

[END OF CONTEXT 7]

HISTORICAL STUDY: EUROPEAN AND WORLD

CONTEXT 8: CAVOUR, GARIBALDI AND THE MAKING OF ITALY, 1815–1870

Answer the following questions using recalled knowledge and information from the sources where appropriate.

Source A is about the failure of the Italian nationalist movement up to 1850.

Source A

> Before 1848 there was little sign of Italian nationalism, except as a wild idea. Mazzini's dream of a democratic republic lost support. The nationalists failed to work together. The revolutionaries of Sicily wanted nothing to do with those of Naples. The revolutionary leaders did not encourage mass participation. The middle classes feared that democratic government would give power to the lower classes. The revolutions were not supported by autocratic leaders, such as King Ferdinand of Sicily.

1. Why did the revolutions of 1848–1849 fail to unite Italy? (Use **Source A** and recall.) **5**

2. Describe the steps taken by Piedmont to bring about Italian unification up to 1860. **5**

Source B was written by a politician in Piedmont in 1861.

Source B

> Count Cavour has the talent to assess a situation and the possibilities of exploiting it. It is this wonderful ability that has helped to bring about a united Italy. Cavour had to seek out opportunities wherever he could. He manipulated events to suit his purpose. He was Prime Minister of an unimportant country so he did not have the resources of a great power like Britain or France.

3. How useful is **Source B** as evidence of the skills of Cavour as a leader? **4**

[END OF CONTEXT 8]

HISTORICAL STUDY: EUROPEAN AND WORLD

CONTEXT 9: IRON AND BLOOD? BISMARCK AND THE CREATION OF THE GERMAN EMPIRE, 1815–1871

Answer the following questions using recalled knowledge and information from the sources where appropriate.

Source A is about the growth of Prussia before 1862.

Source A

> Prussia came to be regarded as the natural leader of a united Germany and therefore emerged as the champion of German nationalism. Prussia controlled the rivers Rhine and Elbe, which were vital communication and trade routes. Other states hoped to benefit from Prussia's industrial development. Prussia took the lead in improving roads and railways. After the revolutions of 1848 Frederick William IV of Prussia promised to work for a united Germany.

1. Why was Prussia able to take the lead in German unification by 1862? (Use **Source A** and recall.) **5**

Source B is from the memoirs of Otto von Bismarck in 1898.

Source B

> I assumed that a united Germany was only a question of time, that the North German Confederation was only the first step in its solution. I did not doubt that a Franco-Prussian War must take place before the construction of a united Germany could be realised. At that time my mind was taken up with the idea of delaying the outbreak of war until our military strength had increased.

2. How useful is **Source B** as evidence of the methods used by Bismarck to bring about the unification of the German states in 1871? **4**

3. Describe the events that led to war between France and Prussia in 1870. **5**

[END OF CONTEXT 9]

HISTORICAL STUDY: EUROPEAN AND WORLD

CONTEXT 10: THE RED FLAG: LENIN AND THE RUSSIAN REVOLUTION, 1894–1921

Answer the following questions using recalled knowledge and information from the sources where appropriate.

Source A explains the treatment of national minorities in the Russian Empire.

Source A

> The diversity of the Empire made it difficult to govern. Many minorities resented the policy of Russification. It made non-Russians use the Russian language instead of their own. Russian style clothes were to be worn and Russian customs were to be adopted. Russian officials were put in to run regional government in non-Russian parts of the Empire like Poland, Latvia and Finland. When Poles complained they were treated as second class citizens, they were told to change and become Russian citizens.

1. Why did national minorities dislike the policy of Russification? (Use **Source A** and recall.) **5**

Source B is from a letter by the leader of the Provisional Government to his parents on 3 July 1917.

Source B

> Without doubt the country is heading for chaos. We are facing famine, defeat at the front and the collapse of law and order in the cities. There will be wars in the countryside as desperate refugees from the cities fight each other for food and land.

2. How useful is **Source B** as evidence of the problems facing the Provisional Government? **4**

3. In what ways did the Civil War affect the Russian people? **5**

[END OF CONTEXT 10]

HISTORICAL STUDY: EUROPEAN AND WORLD

CONTEXT 11: FREE AT LAST? RACE RELATIONS IN THE USA, 1918–1968

Answer the following questions using recalled knowledge and information from the sources where appropriate.

1. Describe the problems facing European immigrants to the USA in the 1920s. **5**

Source A is from a speech made in 1954 by the Grand Dragon of the Federated Klans of Alabama.

Source A

> The Klan don't hate nobody! In fact, the Klan is the black man's best friend. He should behave himself and not allow himself to be fooled by the lies of Northerners. Then he will reap the rewards of hard work, instead of the disappointments of chasing unrealistic dreams!

2. How useful is **Source A** as evidence of attitudes towards Black Americans in the southern states at the time of the Civil Rights movement? **4**

Source B is about the Civil Rights march in Selma, Alabama in 1965.

Source B

> Late in 1964 President Johnson told King that there was little immediate hope that Congress would pass any more Civil Rights legislation. King decided that Johnson, like Kennedy before him, needed a "push". King decided to mount a new protest in Selma, Alabama. The local police chief, Sheriff Clark, was a crude, violent racist. Like Bull Connor he would make a wonderfully obvious enemy. King decided to lead a march from Selma to the state capital Montgomery to protest to Governor George Wallace about police brutality and racism.

3. Why did Martin Luther King plan a Civil Rights protest in Selma, Alabama in 1965? (Use **Source B** and recall.) **5**

[END OF CONTEXT 11]

HISTORICAL STUDY: EUROPEAN AND WORLD

CONTEXT 12: THE ROAD TO WAR, 1933–1939

Answer the following questions using recalled knowledge and information from the sources where appropriate.

1. In what ways did Britain appease Germany between 1933 and 1936? **5**

Source A explains why Germany wanted Anschluss with Austria.

Source A

> The Treaty of Versailles had forbidden unification with Austria. It was obvious that Austria was the key to south eastern Europe, where Germany wanted to spread her influence. Also, Austria had a close relationship with Hungary whom Germany wanted as an ally. Strategically, joining up with Austria would surround western Czechoslovakia and prevent it from being a base for Germany's enemies. Ever since 1918, German governments wanted to unite with Austria. Germany and Austria were joined economically in 1936 so political union was the next logical step.

2. Why did Germany want Anschluss in 1938? (Use **Source A** and recall.) **5**

Source B is from a report by the British ambassador to Germany, August 1938.

Source B

> No matter how badly the Germans behave, we must also condemn Czechoslovakia. No one has much faith in the Czech government's honesty or even their ability to do the right thing over the Sudetenland. We must not blame the Germans for preparing their army because they are convinced that the Czechs want to start a war as soon as possible so they can drag Britain and France into it.

3. How useful is **Source B** as evidence of Britain's attitude to Czechoslovakia in 1938? **4**

[END OF CONTEXT 12]

HISTORICAL STUDY: EUROPEAN AND WORLD

CONTEXT 13: IN THE SHADOW OF THE BOMB: THE COLD WAR, 1945–1985

Answer the following questions using recalled knowledge and information from the sources where appropriate.

Source A explains why the Cold War broke out after 1945.

Source A

> The Allies met at Potsdam in July, 1945. The new American leader, Truman, distrusted the Russians and Stalin did not trust him. Stalin had good reason for being uneasy. While the Allies met at Potsdam a message had reached Truman informing him that America had successfully tested its first atomic bomb. On the 6th of August, the USA dropped an atomic bomb on Hiroshima; three days later, it dropped a second on Nagasaki. Truman had not told Stalin that this was about to happen. Wartime friends, who had fought together to defeat a common enemy, were about to become peacetime enemies.

1. Why did the Cold War break out after 1945? (Use **Source A** and recall.) — **5**

2. Describe the part played by the USSR in the Cuban Missile Crisis. — **5**

Source B is from a speech to the American people by President Reagan in March 1983.

Source B

> Our efforts to rebuild America's forces began two years ago. For twenty years the Soviet Union has been accumulating enormous military might. They didn't stop building their forces, even when they had more than enough to defend themselves. They haven't stopped now. I know that all of you want peace, and so do I. However, the freeze on building nuclear weapons would make us less, not more, secure and would increase the risk of war.

3. How useful is **Source B** as evidence of why the process of détente had come to a halt by the early 1980s? — **4**

[END OF CONTEXT 13]

[END OF PART 3: EUROPEAN AND WORLD CONTEXTS]

[END OF QUESTION PAPER]

[BLANK PAGE]

[BLANK PAGE]

[BLANK PAGE]

[BLANK PAGE]

Acknowledgements

Permission has been sought from all relevant copyright holders and Bright Red Publishing is grateful for the use of the following:

An extract from 'Collins Living History, Medieval Realms, 1066–1500' published by HarperCollins Publishers Ltd © 1992 Christopher Culpin (2006 page 8);

An extract from 'The Coming of the Civil War 1603–49' by D Sharp. Published by Heinemann Educational Publishers. Reproduced by permission of Pearson Education (2006 page 11);

An extract from 'Immigrants and Exiles: Scotland 1830s–1930s' by Sydney Wood, published by Hodder & Stoughton (2006 page 13);

An extract from 'The Crofters' Crown Copyright 1990 The National Archives of Scotland (2006 page 13);

An extract from 'From the Cradle to the Grave: Social Welfare in Britain 1890s–1951' by Simon Wood and Claire Wood, published by Hodder & Stoughton, 2002 (2006 page 14);

An extract from 'Scotland: A Concise History' by Fitzroy MacLean. Copyright © 1970, 1993 and 2000 Thames & Hudson Ltd, London. Reproduced by permission of Thames & Hudson (2006 page 17);

An extract from 'Crusade' by Terry Jones and Alan Ereira, published by BBC books 1996. Reprinted by permission of The Random House Group (2006 page 18);

An extract from 'Voyages of Discovery' by I Gilmour. Reproduced by permission of Pearson Education (2006 page 20);

The photograph 'Ku Klux Klan Marching in Washington' © Bettman/Corbis (2006 page 27);

An extract from 'The Kings and Queens' by Plantagenent Somerset Fry, published by Dorling Kindersley, 1997. Reproduced by permission of Penguin Books Ltd (2007 page 8);

An extract from 'Immigrants and Exiles: Scotland 1830s–1930s' by Sydney Wood, published by Hodder & Stoughton, 2001 (2007 page 13);

An extract from 'From the Cradle to the Grave: Social Welfare in Britain 1890s–1951' by Simon Wood and Claire Wood, published by Hodder & Stoughton, 2002 (2007 page 14);

An adaptation of a memo from District Inspector Spears to the Minister of Home Affairs, 1923, taken from the Public Records Office of Northern Ireland (2007 page 16);

An extract from 'Nationalist and Unionist: Ireland before the Treaty' by T Gray, published by Blackie & Son Ltd, 1990. Reproduced by permission of T Gray (2007 page 16);

An extract from 'The Crusades' by RR Sellman, published by McHuen & Co Ltd, 1968 (2007 page 18);

Adapted extracts from 'Events and Outcomes The Slave Trade' by Tom Monaghan, published by Evans Brothers Ltd (2007 page 22);

An extract from 'Investigating History: Britain 1750–1900', published by Hodder & Stoughton, 2003 (2007 page 22);

An extract from 'Re-discovering Britain 1750–1900' by Andy Reid, Colin Shephard and Dave Martin, published by John Murray, 2001 (2007 page 22);

An extract from 'Free at Last? Race Relations in the USA 1918–1968' by John A Kerr, published by Hodder & Stoughton, 2000 (2007 page 27);

An extract from 'Konclave in Kokomo by Robert Coughlin, taken from 'The Aspirin Age' by Isabel Leighton, published by Simon & Schuster, 1963 (2007 page 27);

An extract from 'History of Britain' by Andrew Langley. Published by Heinemann Educational Publishers, 1996. Reproduced by permission of Pearson Education (2008 page 11);

Two extracts from 'Immigrants and Exiles: Scotland 1830s–1930s' by Sydney Wood, published by Hodder & Stoughton, 2001 (2008 page 13);

An extract from 'Patterns of Migration', published by Scottish Consultative Council on the Curriculum © Learning and Teaching Scotland 2010 (2008 page 13);

An extract from 'From the Cradle to the Grave: Social Welfare in Britain 1890s–1951' by Simon Wood and Claire Wood, published by Hodder & Stoughton, 2002 (2008 page 14);

An extract from 'The Edwardian Age: Complacency and Concern' by Ian B McKellar, published by Blackie & Son, 1980 (2008 page 14);

Extract from 'Colonialism and Colonies', Microsoft Encarta Online Encyclopedia 2008. Reproduced with permission of Microsoft (2008 page 20);

Adapted extracts from 'Events and Outcomes The American Revolution' by Dale Anderson, published by Evans Brother Ltd (2008 page 21);

An extract from 'Black Ivory' by James Walvin, published by Fontana Press, HarperCollins © James Walvin (2008 page 22);

An extract from 'The Unification of Germany 1815–90' by Andrina Stiles, published by Hodder & Stoughton, 1989 (2008 page 23);

An extract from 'Free at Last? Race Relations in the USA 1918–1968' by John A Kerr, published by Hodder & Stoughton, 2000 (2008 page 27);

An extract from 'The Cold War' published by HarperCollins Publishers Ltd © 1996 Fiona MacDonald (2008 page 28);

An extract from 'History of Britain' by Andrew Langley. Published by Heinemann Educational Publishers, 1996. Reproduced by permission of Pearson Education (2009 page 11);

An extract from 'Scotland: A Concise History' by Fitzroy MacLean. Copyright © 1970, 1993 and 2000 Thames & Hudson Ltd., London. Reproduced by permission of Thames & Hudson (2009 page 11);

An extract from 'Highland News, 8th April 1911, reproduced in 'Adventurers and Exiles: The Great Scottish Exodus' by Marjory Harper, published by Profile Books, 2003 (2009 page 13);

An extract from 'From the Cradle to the Grave: Social Welfare in Britain 1890s–1951' by Simon Wood and Claire Wood, published by Hodder & Stoughton, 2002 (2009 page 14);

A cartoon from the Daily Herald newspaper in 1942 © Daily Herald Archive at the National Media Museum/Science & Society Picture Library (2009 page 14);

A poster produced by the Irish National Party in 1915. Courtesy of the National Library of Ireland (2009 page 16);

An extract from 'Understanding Global Issues 10/92 Columbus and after: The beginnings of Colonisation' edited by Richard Buckley, published by European Schoolbooks, 1992 (2009 page 20);

An extract from http://www.en.wikipedia-org/wiki/AgeofDiscovery (2009 page 20);

An extract from 'The Unification of Italy', by Andrina Stiles, published by Hodder & Stoughton, 2006 (2009 page 24);

An extract from 'Cavour, Garibaldi and the Making of Italy 1815–70', published by Scottish Consultative Council on the Curriculum © Learning and Teaching Scotland, 2000 (2009 page 24);

Two extracts from 'Germany 1815–1939' by Jim McGonigle, published by Hodder Gibson 2006 (2009 page 25);

An extract from 'The Growth of Nationalism: Germany and Italy 1815–1939' by Ronald Cameron, Christine Henderson & Charles Robertson, published by Pulse Publications (2009 page 25);

An extract from 'The Civil Rights Movement' by Mark Newman, published by Edinburgh University Press (BAAS Paperbacks) 2004 (2009 page 27);

Two extracts from 'Free at Last? Race Relations in the USA 1918–1968' by John A Kerr, published by Hodder & Stoughton, 2000 (2009 page 27).